Assertiveness

3 Books in 1

-Find Out How Simple Yet Amazingly Powerful Communication Skills Can Shape a Stronger, Deeper & More Fulfilling Relationship in Marriage, for Couples, & Teens Alike

- Skills and Strategies to Effectively Speak Your Mind Without Being Misunderstood

- Useful Methods and Advice to Conquer Small Talk, Improve Social Confidence and Network Like Never Before

Keith Coleman

Table of Contents

COMMUNICATION IN RELATIONSHIPS: FIND OUT HOW SIMPLE YET AMAZINGLY POWERFUL COMMUNICATION SKILLS CAN SHAPE A STRONGER, DEEPER & MORE FULFILLING RELATIONSHIP IN MARRIAGE, FOR COUPLES, & TEENS ALIKE............1

INTRODUCTION 3

CHAPTER 1: VALIDATION DECODED **11**

CHAPTER 2: EMPATHETIC LISTENING **35**

CHAPTER 3: STEPS FOR BOOSTING YOUR EMOTIONAL COMMUNICATION AND EMOTIONAL BIDS **43**

CHAPTER 4: CREATING SHARED MEANING TO BOOST YOUR RELATIONSHIP **55**

CHAPTER 5: CONFLICT RESOLUTION IN RELATIONSHIPS **73**

CONCLUSION **85**

EFFECTIVE COMMUNICATION: *SKILLS AND STRATEGIES TO EFFECTIVELY SPEAK YOUR MIND WITHOUT BEING MISUNDERSTOOD* **87**

INTRODUCTION 89

CHAPTER 1: 13 POWER PACKED TIPS TO ENHANCE YOUR PUBLIC SPEAKING SKILLS AND COMMUNICATE EFFECTIVELY 93

CHAPTER 2: ACTIONABLE BODY LANGUAGE TIPS TO COMPLIMENT YOUR VERBAL SKILLS 109

CHAPTER 3: HOW TO STAY ON THE SAME FOOT WHILE COMMUNICATING WITH PEOPLE 125

CHAPTER 4: USING SPEECH, TONE, AND PITCH TO YOUR ADVANTAGE 137

CHAPTER 5: EFFECTIVE COMMUNICATION IN PERSONAL RELATIONSHIPS 143

CONCLUSION 157

CONVERSATION SKILLS: *USEFUL METHODS AND ADVICE TO CONQUER SMALL TALK, IMPROVE SOCIAL CONFIDENCE AND NETWORK LIKE NEVER BEFORE* 159

INTRODUCTION 161

CHAPTER 1: WHY EFFECTIVE COMMUNICATION SKILLS MATTER 163

CHAPTER 2: COMMUNICATION OBSTACLES YOU'RE LIKELY TO FACE 173

CHAPTER 3: GETTING STARTED ON BUILDING EFFECTIVE CONVERSATION SKILLS........... 185

CHAPTER 4: HOW TO BECOME A CONVERSATIONAL WHIZ AT WORK 195

CHAPTER 5: CHARISMATICALLY COOL 203

CHAPTER 6: CONVERSATIONAL CONFIDENCE IS KEY 213

CONCLUSION 220

Communication in Relationships

Find Out How Simple Yet Amazingly Powerful Communication Skills Can Shape a Stronger, Deeper & More Fulfilling Relationship in Marriage, for Couples, & Teens Alike

Keith Coleman

Introduction

What do people crave the most in a relationship? Of course, they want to be heard. We all want to be listened to and heard. And there's a huge difference between the two. Being a good listener is about clearly physically tuning in to what the other person is saying, but hearing is more about acknowledging and understanding what the person is saying. We've all spoken to a person who clearly hears our words yet doesn't seem to understand what we meant. They may have cognitively understood the point but not connected to it emotionally. Don't we say things like, "I hear you", which implies "I understand what you are trying to convey." That is the kind of hearing we crave for in relationships. One that reveals true connection and understanding! How does one reveal to someone that they are heard? The truly wonderful listeners go beyond listening. They listen, acknowledge, understand and validate the speaker, which makes him/her feel valued.

The most important thing we seek in a relationship is validation. When we talk excitedly about something with our partner, it doesn't mean we love speaking nineteen to a dozen. We are just expecting the person to sense our excitement, and share it. We hope to establish a connection with the person through shared excitement and emotions. The thing that connects us with people is shared emotions and validation.

We make connection bids with people all the time. For example, if we excitedly tell our partner to "just look at this beauty of a car", we don't care so much about the car as much as we crave shared interest and excitement with our partner. We expect the person to respond with shared interest, appreciation, and excitement. These small everyday acts are our way of establishing a connection with our partner. The single most important factor that makes relationships click is validation.

One of the options we have where any problem is concerned is acceptance. Validation is a way for us to communicate acceptance about ourselves and other people. It doesn't necessarily imply agreement and approval. When a close friend or family member make up their mind about something that you don't think is a good decision, validation involves supporting their actions while still keeping a different opinion. It is a way of conveying that the relationship is important even when there are disagreements on various issues. Validation is nothing but recognition, acknowledgment, and acceptance of other people's feelings, emotions, and actions.

At a basic level, all we crave for in relationships is acknowledgment, acceptance, and appreciation, which sewn together culminates into validation.

A person's experiences often influence their emotional reactions. If your partner was bitten by a big dog a few months ago and doesn't like being around your German Shepherd, you say something such as "given your experience with big dogs, I completely understand you not wanting to stay around my pet."

In essence, validation is the act of getting someone to feel not just listened to and heard but also understood. It is about calming someone's fears, concerns and insecurity. Validation can also involve adding to someone's joy, happiness, and excitement, while also quickly resolving disagreements and arguments by keeping the bigger picture in mind.

Most of us may have been in a relationship with a person who may be wonderful at listening but disastrous at validating. While you were relating a challenging experience to them, they will listen with a stoic, unaffected look on their face. Once you are done speaking, they'll come up with something such as, "What else?" Then again, when you are rather stoked and excited about something hoping that they'll share your excitement level, they will listen to you and respond to your animated narration with a poker straight face and something vague like "cool" or "great."

Didn't you simply want to shake up the person and say, "Isn't what I told you exciting enough for you to react to it?" You wait for them to say something like, "That's so amazing" or "I am so excited for you." Essentially, you want the other person to care as much about what you've just shared as you. It acts as a validation for your own emotions, and the shared excitement serves as a connection point for both.

Communication in successful relationships involves generous measures of validation, that you've understood your partner, and that you feel a part of their emotions. When you've been talking for a few minutes in a rather animated and excited, manner, a one-word response from the other person doesn't do much to validate your emotions.

It not always about being a good listener, it's more about offering validation. Some people will actively listen to everything you say. You'll have their attention, they'll seldom interrupt you, and they'll keep aside all other distractions. However, you still won't feel wonderful after talking to them. Why? Because they aren't good at offering validation. Though they tune in to your words, they fail to tune in to the emotions behind the words. They don't connect with or understand the emotions that mark the conversation which explains the blank and frustrating reactions. Healthy communication in relationships involves acceptance and validation.

Let us look at this study helmed by psychologist John Gottman that reinforces the value of validation in relationships. Gottman has studied several thousand couples for the past forty years in an attempt to analyze what makes relationships last and why certain couples have healthier, more fulfilling long lasting bonds while another struggle to maintain it.

Gottman and his co-workers beautified their University of Washington laboratory to look like an elegant and exquisite bed and breakfast. They then sent across invitations to 130 newly married couples to spend time together at the retreat. The watched the couples do things couples typically do on a relaxed weekend or holidays. The couples prepared food, chatted up, cleaned, and generally hung out.

Gottman closely studied and analyzed the communication patterns and interactions between these couples. There emerges a clear pattern. Every now and then, partners would make seemingly insignificant and inconsequential requests for establishing a connection with each other. For instance, the husband would peep out of a window and exclaim, "Wow, look at that car!"

Now, he wasn't simply commenting on the vehicle. He was looking to establish a connection with his partner over a shared interest. He was probably hoping she'd be as excited about the car as he was, and this would serve to be a "connection bid" between the two to strengthen their bond. However momentary or short-lived these connections turn out to be, we are constantly seeking them to strengthen our bond with our partner.

Typically, in the above case, the partner would respond with a "wow, it is indeed wonderful" in positive response case and "ugh, that's just plain hideous" in cases of negative responses.

Then there was the passive response, "Hmm, it's nice." By offering engaging, accepting, and positive responses, we turn towards the speaker while passive and negative responses turn us away from the speaker. Predictably, the way couples reacted to the "connection bids" had a considerable impact on the well-being of their marriage.

Gottman discovered that couples who got divorced during the six-year follow-up duration had only 33 percent turn towards bids (three out of ten of their connection bid requests were received with compassion, excitement, and interest).

On the other hand, couples that remained together after the six-year duration had turned towards bids a staggering 87 percent of the time. Almost nine out of ten times, their connection bids met with positive responses. Couples in healthy relationships responded to their partner's emotional requirements. Simply by observing these interactions and communication patterns, Gottman is able to predict with about 94 percent accuracy whether couples with break up, stay together and be unhappy, stay together and be happy, and more several years from now.

If you are making multiple connection bids throughout the day, and your partner is only responding to them positively or turning in towards you positively for a fraction of the time, it may be time to reevaluate the relationship.

What exactly is this turning in towards a person? Turning towards a person is simply a way of describing validation. It is about revealing an interest in and offering affirmation for the other person's requests, feelings, interests, and excitement. You are demonstrating your understanding of their emotions and agreeing to be a part of these emotions.

The insights presented in this book will help you realize how critical validation is when it comes to building and nurturing healthy, satisfying and fulfilling relationships. These strategies can be applied to romantic and other relationships. You'll learn not just how to be a good listener but also a fantastic validator.

Chapter 1:

Validation Decoded

Now that we realize how important validation is in a relationship, it is important to know how one can go about validating effectively in a relationship to strengthen the connection. Validation in relationships has two fundamental components such as identifying a specific emotion and proving justification for experiencing the emotion.

Let us say you are trying to talk to your partner at the end of a long and stressful day. You can tell that they are affected by something. So you inquire if things are alright with them. Suddenly, a volcano of emotions come surging through. "You know this project manager of mine makes me do all the back-breaking work and takes away all the credit for reports and projects which I've worked really hard to put together. He doesn't even acknowledge my efforts or even praise me. This has become a pattern now, and it's driving me insane. I just don't feel driven enough to do good work anymore."

In such a scenario, most people will be tempted to offer assurance, suggestions, and advice. However, research in relationships reveals that it helps to validate the person's emotions first before you slip into the advice-offering mode. Assurance and advice come later, validation comes first. So the best possible response can be something such as "Really? That's insane. It would drive me nuts too." This is validating your partner's emotions. It tells them that you understand how they feel and that they are right in feeling the way they do. You reveal you understand where exactly they are coming from. In short, you are offering them appreciation, acceptance, and respect, which immediately strengthens the connection. Can validation truly be the clincher? Try it, you'll be surprised by the results.

There are innumerable validating responses. As long as the person knows that you recognize, understand and accept their emotions, you are on track with your validation mission. Here are some typical validation responses; "Wow, now that would be perplexing"; "She said that to you? I'd be fuming too if someone said it to me"; "This is truly sad"; "You should be proud of yourself. It's a huge accomplishment"; and "I am delighted for you. You've worked so hard for this. It must surely be an amazing feeling." Observe how every response refers to a clear emotion that offers some justification for the person's emotions or reveals acceptance for their feelings. Both these attributes demonstrate to the other person that you aren't just hearing them but also understanding them.

While it is important to understand and analyze validating responses, it is as important to go over invalidating responses. Often, these responses are harmless and originate from positive intentions. However, they don't add value to the relationship. Invalidating responses often dismiss the other person's emotions. You reveal to the other person that they aren't really right in feeling the way they do, thus leading to the minimization of their emotions.

Typical invalidating responses will be; "You'll be okay"; "Things could've been worse"; "That's not a big deal"; "Don't stress. Things will fall in place"; "At least so and so didn't happen"; and "Smile and rough it out." These responses can worsen the situation even though they may be said with the right intentions. It reveals that the speaker is not right in thinking or feeling the way they do. Though this isn't said directly, the other person is made to feel that they are being irrational or they shouldn't feel this way.

This is the opposite of what they are trying to accomplish by speaking to you. By talking to you, the person is trying to seek validation for your feelings. They are trying to garner reinforcement that they are right in feeling the way they do. Consciously learn to tune in to your responses and modify them into more validating ones if you want more fulfilling, rewarding, and gratifying relationships. You'll be blown by the difference this one tiny change can make in your relationship.

Though we think we mean well by offering suggestions and advice, it serves counterproductive to the process of validating a person's emotions. By offering suggestions and advice, you dismiss their emotions. One of the deepest human desires is to be understood. True understanding isn't possible without generous measures of empathy. "We all want to be with a person who hears us without being judgmental, without taking responsibility for us, and without trying to shape or mold us," as Carl Rogers aptly said. Go back to an instance where you felt truly heard. What did your partner do to make you feel that he/she understood your emotions or why you feel the way you do? This validated your feelings and led you to develop a closer bond with the person.

Tips for Emotionally Validating a Person

Emotional validation is about learning and understanding or expressing acceptance of an individual's emotional experiences. The opposite of emotional validation can be emotional invalidation, where another person's emotional experiences are completely overlooked, rejected, or judged. In short, you are making the person feel that he/she is wrong in feeling the way they do. This creates a sort of emotional disconnect between the two partners.

One of the most critical factors to keep in mind when it comes to validating other people's emotions is that it does not necessarily involve you agreeing with the other person or your belief that they are right in feeling the way they do. Rather, you are communicating to them that you understand what they are feeling even if you don't necessarily agree with it. There is no attempt to talk them out of experiencing it or induce shame for feeling the way they do.

Here are some master tips for validating a person's emotions to forge stronger bonds and a deeper connection.

1. Recognize and acknowledge the emotion.

When you attempt to validate a person's emotional response or experience, the first step is acknowledging the emotion. This can be slightly challenging if the other person is not able to clearly express his/her feelings. You may have to probe further to identify exactly how they are feeling. It can also involve some amount of guesswork, and reframing what they said to check your understanding.

Imagine that your partner is upset with you. You get back from work, and they are demonstrating behavior that reveals they are angry. If they express feelings of being angry openly, your response can be something such as, "I understand you are upset or angry."

On the other hand, if they are simply acting angry, you can say something such as "You appear angry, is everything okay?", or "You look angry, what is happening?"

2. Acknowledging the source of their emotion.

The second step is to recognize or identify the main source of their emotion. What is the clue or situation that is causing them to experience the emotion? For instance, you may inquire, "What is causing you to feel the way you do?"

At times, the person may not be able to clearly express what is triggering the specific emotion in them. Hell, they may not even know it themselves. Other times, they may be unwilling to share it openly or hesitate to reveal the triggers that are causing them to feel the way they do. In such a scenario, you go with the knowledge that something is causing them to feel the emotion. You communicate to them that you are really eager to know why they are feeling the way they do but it is tough for you without a clear understanding of the situation.

3. Validating the emotion.

Now, imagine that your partner or loved one can convey the source of their feelings. They express that they are angry because they feel you are not spending enough time with them. To you, them being upset or angry feels completely unwarranted because you are working to give your family a good life. However, remember what I said earlier about good validation skills. Even when you don't necessarily agree with the person, you understand why they feel the way they do. You communicate that you accept and understand what they are feeling even if you don't agree with their reasoning.

For example, you may say something such as, "I know you are angry because you feel I don't spend enough time with you. However, it isn't my intention to upset you. I was occupied with a huge project which will propel my career in the right direction. I can see that not spending enough time with me made you upset." Don't apologize for your behavior if you don't think you are wrong. But don't fail to acknowledge the other person's feelings. This way you will end up diffusing a potentially volatile situation. The person will feel a lot calmer when you accept their right to feel the way they do instead of trying to justify your actions, thus proving them wrong in feeling a particular emotion.

Here's what validation *is not*, just so you know:

Validation doesn't involve making the emotions go away.

Validating a partner or loved one's emotions doesn't imply that those emotions will go away. It may temporarily diffuse a volatile situation but beyond that, the emotion per se still stays. The situation may not get any worse. However, it doesn't mean the person will feel much better immediately. Keep in mind that it's not your responsibility to drive away the other person's feelings, though you can be supportive. Identifying, acknowledging, and validating their emotions may help them come up with a way to deal with or manage their emotions more effectively.

Validation doesn't mean giving up.

Validation doesn't imply that you are resigning yourself to be treated disrespectfully or badly. If your partner or loved one becomes aggressive or displays inappropriate behavior, distance yourself from the situation. Validating the other person doesn't mean you allow yourself to be treated poorly. Let a person know that you desire to talk to them about the situation. However, it isn't possible to talk about it in a healthy and productive manner until they learn to communicate more calmly. Leave some gap, and return when the time is right.

Six Levels of Validation

Learning how to give validation more mindfully and effectively takes consistent practice and effort. To be an even more competent validator, use Marsha Linehan's (Ph. D) six levels of validation.

Level One – Be Present

The first level of validation involves being present. There are innumerable ways to reinforce your presence. It can range from holding a person's hand when they are feeling particularly distressed to giving them complete attention while they are talking by putting everything aside to empathize with them when they are pouring their heart out.

Multi-tasking, while the person is speaking, is not a sign of being present or aware. Being present is giving 100 percent attention to the speaker you are attempting to validate. Being present involves acknowledging your experience, and dealing with it rather than scooting in the other direction. You basically learn to sit with or manage intense emotions even if they feel uncomfortable for a while.

Often, people are uncomfortable with extreme emotions because they don't know how to acknowledge it. We are at a loss of words about how best to comfort someone experiencing intense emotions. Just be present, and pay attention to the individual in nonjudgmental ways. Where your emotions are concerned, be mindful and accept them.

Level Two – Validation is Accurate Reflection

Accurate reflection involves summarizing what we've heard from the other person or summarizing your feelings about it. When it is done in a genuine manner, with the intention of understanding a person's experience without judging it, this accurate reflection is validation. At times, reflection helps differentiate emotions from logical thoughts. A person may say something like, "I am angry and terribly hurt." This can be an example of self-reflection. Your reaction to this can be something such as, "It sounds like you are upset because you didn't reach out to them again." You help the other person separate their feelings from logical thoughts.

Level Three – Mindreading

Mindreading, as the term suggests, is guessing about how the person is feeling or how they are thinking. People do not always understand themselves correctly. They grapple to come to terms with their feelings, emotions, and thoughts. For instance, some people may confuse happiness and enthusiasm or excitement. Some people won't really be clear about the feelings they are experiencing because they may have been conditioned to be fearful or hesitant about openly expressing their emotions.

People may hide their emotions because they may have learned that others do not react positively or sensitively to their emotions. This hiding or masking of emotions means the person is incapable of acknowledging their emotions even to themselves. This makes it all the more challenging for them to regulate or manage their emotions.

When your partner or loved one is discussing a situation, closely observe their emotional state through verbal and non-verbal clues. They may not be able to clearly express what they are feeling. However, if you tune in to their body language, tone, and expressions, you may be able to read their mind to know exactly how they are feeling.

You can say something such as, "I guess you must be feeling pretty upset about the fact that your boss chose to rebuke you in front of everyone present." Keep in mind that your guess could be incorrect. It's the other person's feelings and emotions, and only they are in a position to tell how they are feeling. If the person corrects you, accepting their correction is also a form of validation.

Level Four – Understanding Behavior Based on Biology and History

Our experiences along with biology largely determine our emotional reactions. If your partner has been terribly betrayed in a past relationship, they may not trust you easily. In such a situation, validation can involve saying something such as "Given what happened to you in the previous relationship, I understand that you will take time to trust me."

Level Five – Normalizing Emotional Reactions

Understand that the other person's feelings are normal is valuable to the process of validation. For a person who is more emotionally sensitive, recognizing that a person will be upset in a given situation is validation. For instance, "Of course, you are upset. Addressing an audience for the first time can be nerve-wracking for anyone."

Level Six – Radical Genuineness

Radical genuineness involves understanding the feeling a person is experiencing at a deeper level. You may have experienced something similar. Radical genuineness comprises sharing the person's experiences as an equal.

You may correctly comprehend the levels of validation. However, implementing it is more challenging. Consistent practice is the key to naturally incorporating validation while communicating with your partner and loved ones.

Let's take an example to determine which level of validation can be used in different scenarios. Your closest buddy is angry and upset that her partner destroyed her credit card due to her overspending habit. She is upset that he is controlling her life and making her feel like an irresponsible child. How do you validate her feelings in such a situation?

You can use level two validation for saying something such as, "I understand you are angry because your partner cut up your credit card without your consent. This made you feel like your opinion didn't matter or that you were being treated like an irresponsible child." You reflect the thoughts, feelings, and emotions back to the person; thus, you demonstrate your acceptance of the person's emotional experiences.

You can't use radical genuineness as it is not likely that you have similar experiences, which means that you may not be able to understand or relate to their feelings at a deeper level. This means you may not have a similar emotional reaction or experience. Level five or normalizing the emotional reaction may not help because most people will agree that the reaction was reasonable and avoid being upset in a similar situation. There is nothing in terms of biology or history to be able to relate to the person more effectively, so the level isn't possible. There is no guesswork involved, so level three is also out of question.

Let us look at yet another example to understand the point more effectively. Mary tells you that she quit her job because her managers were constantly taking credit for all the hard work she was putting in to create exceptional projects. She urged them to give her due credit on previous occasions. However, her requests fell on deaf ears. She couldn't continue to work in an environment where her efforts weren't acknowledged and appreciated, and someone else took the entire credit for it. What validation level do you think is most appropriate in such a scenario?

A level five or six validation may work effectively in such a scenario. If you have experienced something similar or being in a similar situation, you may be able to relate to how she is feeling. You may say something such as, "I understand how you feel. I would've taken the same decision." This is level six validation. On the other hand, level five validation can be something like, "I think most people experience the same feelings, emotions, and thoughts that you are experiencing." In level five validation, you are reinforcing that the person's emotional reactions and responses are normal even though you may not have experienced it yourself. In other words, you are normalizing their feelings and emotions.

Although the person may have a history of not being treated well or not receiving their due, you don't use level four. As a rule of thumb, one uses the highest possible level of validation.

What Is Emotional Invalidation?

As important as it is to know what we must do to validate other person's feelings and emotions as part of our communication pattern in relationships, it is also important to understand emotional invalidation. You know what not to do if you've been unknowingly incorporating it in your communication pattern.

Emotional invalidation is when an individual's thoughts, emotions, and feelings are completely rejected, judged or overlooked. While emotional invalidation can be distressing for anyone, it is particularly upsetting for someone who is sensitive. Emotional disruption creates an emotional disconnect and distance from the other person. Even the most well-intentioned people can end up invalidating their partner or loved one's feelings. Though it may not occur intentionally, some people are incapable of dealing with intense emotions. At times, they believe that they are helping the other by offering guidance, suggestions, and advice. In the process, they end up invalidating other people's feelings.

For example, when you are feeling upset or sad, your loved one or partner may say something such as, "Come on now, don't feel sad. Do you want some candy to feel better?" This sounds like a well-meaning way to get someone who is feeling low into a more positive frame of mind. However, it can be highly invalidating for the other person at a deeper, subconscious level. By saying something like this, you are disregarding or dismissing their emotions as something that can be fixed with some candy. In your bid to make someone feel happier and less upset, we often up invalidating their thoughts and emotions.

An effort to get them to feel better can follow acknowledging and validating their emotions. You can begin by identifying and validating how they feel, followed by offering advice for helping them feel better. This is a more well-rounded process, which acknowledges their emotions and offers them a plan of action to deal with these emotions.

What Are the Different Ways Through Which We Invalidate Emotions?

Blaming - "You are such a crybaby to be affected by such insignificant issues and ruining our vacation." This is a classic case of invalidating the other person's feelings and thoughts by blaming them for feeling the way they do. "You always make things harder for me without thinking about it logically." Again, a typically invalidating statement that attempts

Judging – Judging invalidating statements will be something such as, "You are overreacting to the situation," or "That is an absolutely ridiculous thought." You are ridiculing the person's emotions and thoughts.

Minimizing – "Don't worry, it isn't anything as big as you feel it is," or "Don't stress yourself over nothing." These statements are usually said with the right intentions. However, it sends across the message that they are not right in feeling the way they do.

Nonverbal validation – Nonverbal validation can be even more damaging than verbal validation. It can include everything from tapping fingers on a surface to pointing your feet away from the speaker to rolling eyes. Something as seemingly harmless as checking your phone or the time on your watch while someone is speaking can be non-verbal invalidation. Whether you intend to send the message or not, playing a game on your phone or fidgeting with an object can be a sign of non-verbal invalidation.

The best way to convert invalidation from validation is to consciously incorporate validation in your daily communication with your partner or loved ones. The best strategy for preventing invalidation of other people's emotions doesn't involve lying or agreeing with the speaker. It is simply about accepting their internal emotions, experiences, and thoughts as valid. This paves the way for a powerful connection between you and another person.

Tips for Validating a Person's Thoughts, Emotions, and Experiences

1. Offer verbal responses to show you're mentally present and listening.

Validation begins by incorporating fundamental listening skills. It is vital to periodically give short yet effective verbal responses reinforcing the fact that you are hearing them. Say things such as, "okay", "I see", "hmm", "uh-huh", "ahaa" and so on. It shows the other person that you are listening to them and acknowledging their emotions. The person feels heard when you use brief yet effective acknowledgment responses. Things like, "I see where you are coming" or "I hear you" is also effective in reinforcing your understanding of their thoughts and emotional experiences.

2. Be more present and mindful.

The most fundamental validation form is staying with a person mentally, even when their feelings are intense, uncomfortable, challenging to handle or unpleasant. We keep aside our discomfort and concentrate on being physically and mentally present for the other person. There are many ways to show you are present and listening to your partner or loved one. It can be holding their hand to demonstrate your support or looking them in the eyes while they are speaking. It can also involve rubbing their back or lightly touching their shoulder to show support. Other signals of 'I am always there for you' involve placing your open palm over the other person's palm, running your hand over their head, and running your hand over their upper hand.

3. Respond to the other person's overall mood, vibe, and energy level.

One of the best ways to reveal validation (remember Gottman's research?) is to match the other person's energy, vibe, and excitement levels. If your partner is excited about something, make an attempt to mirror their excitement. If they appear upset or disappointed, match their sense of disappointment. Mirroring a person's vibe and energy levels while responding to their feelings and emotions makes them feel like they are understood.

For instance, let us say your partner is excited about a new job offer in a different city. He/she may appreciate you getting as excited about it or revealing your happiness for their success. On the contrary, if your partner isn't sure or slightly tentative about moving to another city, and you are hyper excited about it, they may feel overwhelmed or smothered. Read the person emotions accurately and frame your responses to match it.

4. Seek clarification.

When a person finishes talking and expressing their feelings, ask questions to clarify your understanding of their emotional experiences. This will give you more insights into their emotions and thoughts. Also, it is an opportunity for the speaker to elaborate on their emotions, feelings, and thoughts in a manner where they feel heard and understood.

For instance, say something such as, "So what do you feel about this?" or "How did you feel when that happened?" Giving the other person an opportunity to elaborate on their emotional experiences shows them that you care about or are interested in what they are saying.

Use body language and non-verbal signals to demonstrate that you are tuned in to what the person is saying as well as what they leave unsaid. Closely observe a person while they are speaking. Stop everything else and look at the person while they are speaking to pick up verbal and non-verbal clues. Frequently look at a person, nod your head, and uncross your hands and legs along with other clues to demonstrate you are paying attention.

Avoid being preoccupied with your own thoughts or keep aside your own level of discomfort by focusing on being there for a person.

5. Repeat the person's words and actions to offer validation.

After a person has expressed their feelings, emotions, and thoughts, repeat their words and phrases to mirror their state of mind and reinforce your understanding of their emotional experiences. Initially, it may feel slightly silly. However, this validates their emotional experiences and thoughts effectively. It demonstrates to the speaker that you've heard and understood them.

Try saying something such as, "So you are upset that the lecturer gave you a little warning about not accepting your project"; "Wow, you look so excited, and I am so happy for you"; "This must be really hard for you"; and "Help me understand this correctly. You felt hurt that my friend mimicked your friend and called him a few names, while I didn't say anything, right?"

6. Listen more and speak less.

Validating involves more listening and less speaking. You can listen to, acknowledge, identify, and validate a person's emotional experiences unless you listen to them. Avoid the urge to constantly offer suggestions and advice to the speaker. This makes them feel like you aren't acknowledging their emotions or offering superficial responses. Instead, concentrate on listening to the person and being around for them. A majority of times, people get their own revelations about a particular situation or issue when you just tune out of everything else and lend them a listening ear.

7. Help the person elaborate on his/her feelings.

After your partner or loved one has expressed their feelings, gently help them elaborate on how they are feeling and the reason behind feeling the way they do. For example, you can say something such as, "I can imagine how upset you must be?" This demonstrates to another person that their feelings are important to you and that you are trying your best to understand them.

If your understanding of their emotional experiences is accurate, they will say something like, "Yes that's right and ..." Thus, they will go on to elaborate on their feelings and pour their heart out to you. If your reading of their thoughts and emotions is incorrect, they may come with something like, "No, actually it is like this ..." and go on to correct your understanding of the situation or issue. Both ways, you are offering an opportunity to the other person to elaborate on their thoughts, feelings, and emotions.

8. Recall your own similar experiences.

This is another fantastic validation tip that can leave the other person feel much better. Wherever possible (while being genuine and authentic), demonstrate to the person that you understand how they feel or relate to their emotional experience because you've been through something similar too. Go back to how you ended up feeling, and how their feelings are completely understandable. This helps validate their emotional experiences.

For instance, lets us say your partner didn't get invited to brother's vacation and is upset about it, you can say something like, "Yes, loneliness can be tough. My sister and cousins go on a vacation every year, and I am never invited because I am a few years older than them. It disappoints me that I am left out of the fun. I totally understand how you must be feeling upset about not getting invited to your brother's thing. It is hurtful to be alone and left out."

9. Normalize the person's reaction.

Even if you haven't experienced something similar, you can help validate a loved one's feelings or emotional experiences by saying something such as, "I think a majority of people would feel the way you are feeling right now too." This validates to them that their reactions are completely reasonable, and they are right in feeling the way they do. You can use some of these normalizing statements for validating a person's behavior. "It is alright to get squeamish about your vaccination. No one enjoys them", or "of course you are nervous as hell about your first presentation. It can make the best of us jittery", and "no wonder you are so upset. Anyone would be if their boss criticizes them publically."

10. Acknowledging the person's history.

You can validate a person's feelings by acknowledging how they feel based on their history and past experiences. Pro tip: this is more valuable when your partner or loved one is worried about coming across as unreasonable, illogical, or irrational about their emotions and thoughts. Even if the person is reacting in a slightly over the top manner, you can reach out to them and demonstrate your understanding of their emotional experiences by saying something like, "Given how Jess treated you, I completely understand why you would want to sign a prenup before we get married. It isn't wrong to watch out for your own interests, especially after what you are recovering from", or "After being bitten by that scary looking dog down the street last year, it is understandable that my dog makes you nervous."

Chapter 2:

Empathetic Listening

One of the most important components of validation involves listening empathetically to your partner. Empathy is the cornerstone of listening to and understanding the person.

Have you just wanted your other half to listen to you instead of offering suggestions, advice, and solutions?

Haven't we all at some point experienced the frustration of our partner's inability to empathize with our feelings?

Empathetic listening is the basis of validation, which in turn is the secret ingredient for healthy, rewarding, and fulfilling relationships. Although empathetic listening is integral to the success of interpersonal relationships, it doesn't come easy. However, when you care enough to understand the other person's point of view, you will make an attempt to listen to them.

The main idea is that empathy for a human being can be as crucial as say their physical safety even though it may not be as apparent. We seek empathy and understanding in our relationships as much as we seek physical safety in life. This has been going on since our primordial days, and evolution hasn't changed much of it. Human beings are wired at a biological level for deriving attunement from other human beings. It equals survival for them, which is why we are as concerned about receiving it as we are about our physical survival.

Therefore, get ditch the habit of offering suggestions and advice when your partner is talking to you. Say this as many times as it takes to get embedded into your subconscious mind — validation wins over solutions. However well-meaning our efforts may be to fix things for our partner or loved ones, lending them an empathetic ear matters more than getting into ninja fix-it mode! Even when solutions are clearly visible, wait for the right timing. When someone pours their hearts out to you, all they are looking for a listening ear, not fix-its or suggestions (however well-meaning they are).

Why does empathetic listening matter? A feeling of being felt is a large part of our emotional connection in interpersonal relationships. Even when our perceptions of a situation differ, on a primitive level, we all seek to be understood from our viewpoint. This is even truer for distressing and negative emotions. We need to feel the safety and comfort of knowing that our loved ones will understand how we feel. Without this factor, relationships are almost always likely to crumble. Emotional connections are vital to the survival of a relationship.

Empathetic listening gives us an opportunity to establish emotional connects with our partners and loved ones to help them feel acknowledged and understood. It tells our partners that are we are more than willing to listen to them in a non-judgmental and open manner while understanding where they are coming from.

Think of you and your partner holding a joint emotional connection account. Each time you listen to them empathetically, there is a credit in your joint emotional connection account (which is great for you too). On the other hand, each time you do not practice empathetic listening, there is a debit from your joint emotional connection account (thus you lose too when the connection becomes weak). These deposits can be dipped into when we need them later.

Here are some ways to boost your empathetic listening skills.

1. Be non-judgmental.

It isn't easy for you to listen to your partner or loved ones without offering your take on it because you happen to closely know the person. However, instead of focusing on the person's actions or decisions, focus on their emotional experiences. Focus on their perspective or try to understand where they are coming from. This doesn't mean you necessarily agree with everything the person says. It simply demonstrates to them that you support them and care about their feelings.

The next time your partner, a close friend, or family member pours their heart out to you, resist the urge to give your take on it and instead, attempt to understand their perspective. You may or may not agree with the person. However, you try to understand where they are coming from by acknowledging and offering reinforcement for their feelings without judging them. Resist the urge to chip in with your two cents. Chances are they're not looking for your take on the matter. They only want their take on the matter to be acknowledged, understood, and validated. This is a major reason for disconnects in interpersonal relationships. People often jump in with their views without attempting to understand how the other person is feeling. In a bid to be heard, everyone stops hearing. This leads to frustration and a general feeling of not being understood by our partner or loved ones.

For example, your partner may share their feelings about a friend who keeps cutting them off in the middle of a conversation and playing one up on them when they go out together as a group. As a concerned partner, you may feel a compelling urge to get into solution-offering-mode by saying something like, "You must talk to him/her about it. I think he/she is jealous of you." Chances are, they already know this and are not seeking a solution. All the person wants is for you to understand how she/he feels when they are constantly being cut off or at the receiving end of one-upmanship games played by a so-called friend.

2. Give the person undivided attention.

There are no two ways about it. Empathetic listening involves eliminating distractions to ensure you spend time listening to the person mindfully, purposefully, and intentionally. Giving a loved one undivided attention signifies respect, concern, and interest in what they are saying. Also, the other is likelier to keep calm when they're respected and understood. Being present in the truest sense of the term is integral to the process of offering the speaker our undivided attention. If you are someone who is constantly checking their phone or emails, work on putting everything aside to the give the other person undivided attention.

3. Tune in to facts and feelings.

Soak in the logical as well as emotional bits of the other person's speech. What is the larger view or emotion the person is trying to convey? What are the facts and figures within their narrative? Are there any clues that you need to tune in to better understand what they are saying? To practice empathetic listening, one needs to listen with one's ears, eyes, and soul.

4. Let the other person know that you are listening to them.

Think about your verbal and nonverbal signals. Complement these words with non-verbal gestures such as maintaining eye contact, nodding, leaning towards the speaker. All these are non-verbal clues that signal attentiveness at a subconscious level. Listen to the person without interrupting him or her.

5. Silence is integral to the process of empathetic listening.

Sometimes, all an individual needs are to be heard and know that you are physically as well as mentally present when they are speaking. There will be moments of silence when the person is reflecting upon their feelings or contemplating what to say next, which means there will be moments of silence throughout the conversation. Avoid trying to fill these seemingly awkward silences. Don't immediately jump in to respond.

Give the other person a few seconds of silence to get a hold of their emotions, and determine how to best express them. You can't and shouldn't always rescue people. Don't play knight in shining armor each time your partner or loved ones shares a distressing situation with you. Like most adults, they are fully capable of making their own choices and navigating their way through life. Eventually, they will find their way out through the toughest situations. Right now when they are operating on 'raw emotions' mode, all they need is an understanding ear. Give it to them and you've won their heart.

Of course, you are there for support should they need it. However, avoid the urge to do anything other than understanding how they are feeling and letting them know they have your support. Allow the person to go over their own emotions while they are speaking to you. What happens is that when a person is recounting their feelings or emotional experiences in a specific situation, they are also reinforcing these feelings to themselves. It is also like having a conversation with yourself while clarifying certain emotional experiences and thoughts to oneself. This makes the person feel much better and relieved, which helps him to establish a meaningful connection with the listener. The positive feelings of reinforcing one's feelings of himself/herself and the other person help build a connection between the speaker and the listener.

6. Paraphrase and restate what the other person is saying.

Refer to the speaker's words, ask questions, and use clarifying comments as required. Keep your approach nonjudgmental, respectful, and based on the person's energy. For example, "If I understand you correctly, you are upset that your manager criticized you publically without giving you a chance to air your side of the story." You are summarizing or paraphrasing what the person just said for two reasons:

- To show the other person that you've been listening to him/her.
- To confirm your understanding of the other person's emotions so you can correct your stance if you are incorrect in your understanding.

Don't launch into a verbose story mode. Just summarize what the person said in a brief and succinct manner, so the other person knows you've understood them and have an opportunity to correct you if you've misunderstood what they are trying to communicate.

Chapter 3:

Steps for Boosting Your Emotional Communication and Emotional Bids

Using body language (and other non-verbal) communication to your benefit comprises picking up several clues that the person offers through their expressions, posture, walk, gestures, and more to interpret what they are feeling and what they leave unsaid. For instance, your partner may tell you they've had a "good day" but their body language may indicate stress and frustration. If you are quick to catch on emotional communication clues, you will know exactly how your partner is feeling, and tailor your response accordingly to recognize, acknowledge, and validate their feelings.

Most conflicts in interpersonal relationships occur when a person is unable to gather clues about their partner's state of mind and hence cannot determine the course of their response. Whether it is helping a close friend deal with the stress of work or asking your steady date to marry you, gauging the situation and adapting to it with a satisfactory emotional reaction is integral to handling the situation. When the friend feels good after your reassuring words, you'll know it is time to stop. If your date doesn't appear to be in good mood, you'll know it is time to hold off the conversation for another day.

These are two examples of when we can read other people's emotions and communicate in a befitting manner by considering the other person's feelings, thoughts, and emotions. There are countless instances when you interact to communicate and interpret each other's emotions. The more adept you become at communicating and reading emotional responses, the more fulfilling and meaningful these interactions will be.

No two marriages or relationships are even remotely similar if you ask any experienced marriage therapist. Couples come together in the unlikeliest, most wonderful, and strangest situations. Some may have similar struggles but in different ways. Every relationship is distinct with its own set of dynamics, which also involves different conflict management strategies. Similarly, every couple has different dreams and visions about the future. However, couples that have maximum fun, and share more meaningful bonds are ones who are successfully able to create shared meaning.

Enquire with any artist about what drives them to be creative, they'll tell you being creative is about being messy, joyous, fun, adventurous, risky, elusive, maddening, stimulating, intriguing, and invigorating. This isn't any different in relationships. A relationship is pretty much a work of art. You have to keep on being imaginative, reinvent, and come up with innumerable ways to keep the relationship alive (similar to creating new works of art) as you move together through life. Find some guideposts to creating shared meaning on the way.

Why Is Emotional Communication Significant in Relationships?

Though it is one of the most important life skills, emotional communication is seldom taught to us in school or college. This is why plenty of people struggle to develop an understanding of other people's feelings and emotions while communicating with them. Emotions play a huge role in the process of communication. When we tune in to our and other people's emotions, the interaction turns out to be even more effective. Emotional awareness of the ability to comprehend our own emotions helps while communicating with others. Emotionally aware folks make for better and more impactful communicators, especially in interpersonal relationships. You will quickly identify the emotions of your partner or loved one, along with the feelings that impact their communication patterns. You will understand what the other person is communicating even more effectively.

Here are six brilliant ways to strengthen your emotional communication with your partner or loved one to enjoy more rewarding relationships.

1. Share small insignificant experiences instead of just speaking about it.

One of the golden rules for strengthening your emotional connection and communication with your partner involves not just speaking about small and seemingly insignificant experiences but also sharing them. A recent research in the Psychological Science suggests that we experience greater intimacy with people when we speak about common experiences.

For instance, a couple facing challenges in their relationships can take the initial step towards rebuilding their relationship by speaking about their kids, especially those related to pleasant shared moments or endearing incidents. When couples are encouraged to speak about happy moments together with their children collectively, it is almost always with the objective of repairing a damaged relationship. Talking about their shared experiences with their children helps them experience a close emotional connection, thus strengthening their bond.

In the above example, since conflicts almost happen around nurturing families, one has to be careful that moments which trigger discord aren't brought up. These shared experiences can seldom be expressed to their fullest in words. Another research conducted by Psychological Science revealed that words aren't required for a couple's shared emotions and feelings to enhance a relationship. Merely doing something together where they can both partake the same experience such as going on a bike ride, catching a movie together, sharing a dessert, and so on can intensify their pleasant experiences, thus leading to an improvement in their bond through these shared pleasant experiences.

Do something small at the same time to boost your bonds. A tiny action can be worth more than a thousand words if done at the right time with the right intention. Something as simple as reaching out for your partner's arm while catching a movie together or briefly making contact with your body (for a few seconds) by leaning against the other person can make a huge difference to the bond. At times, speaking about intimacy can take away from the joy of it. Share actions and small moments of intimacy through shared experiences in silence instead of talking about it. It will instantly strengthen your emotional communication with your partner.

2. Increase these shared experiences on a daily basis.

Once you are able to identify these seemingly insignificant yet precious shared moments with your partner, find ways to incorporate these actions, experiences, and moments in your daily life as a couple. If any of the partners are not adept at expressing themselves in words or describing commonplace daily details, fret not. Do not worry about not being able to express mundane details. Instead, make time for doing insignificant, meaningless, and unimportant activities together such as watching television together, listening to your favorite songs, going grocery shopping, doing laundry together, and so on. These actions are more critical on an everyday basis than simply talking about your day. Of course, people who are expressive and articulate about their feelings will have more open and meaningful conversations with their partners. However, focus on creating shared experiences and memories around small events on a daily basis to strengthen your bond as a couple.

3. Small talk can be big when it comes to boosting relationships.

Small talk isn't just a way to break the ice with strangers or get to know people in a business networking event. It can be brilliantly used to strengthen emotional connections in interpersonal relationships too. Insignificant details and small talk are supposedly more effective for building strong emotional ties with your partner than the seemingly deep discussions about emotions and feelings.

Harry Sullivan, an American psychoanalyst, formulated an approach that he termed "detailed injury." It suggests that therapists gather details about every aspect of a client's life. Through these small details, Sullivan believes he can determine who a person truly is. Gottman's research that we discussed in the earlier chapter concluded that it is often the mundane and fleeting everyday moments that affect the nature of interpersonal relationships. The more emotionally meaningful, charged, and serious conversations do not impact the health of our relationship as much as the seemingly mundane details.

Instead of being bored when your partner is recounting the details of a plumbing issue or a game they watched last night, reveal an interest in it. We often believe that we know all the details about our partner's life. However, according to Gottman, it's a way for couples to get closer. Something as seemingly mundane as making a to-do list together during a home renovation job can be a way of demonstrating your affection and fondness for each other. You may incorporate your partner's suggestions and preferences (that they'd probably mentioned off-hand a while ago and you remember) without asking them. These small gestures reveal that you care enough for them to do small things that bring them comfort, happiness, and joy.

On the face of it, you may feel like inquiring may seem intrusive, offensive, rude and critical. Bear in mind that you are not playing FBI and questioning them to catch them doing wrong. By asking these questions, you are letting the other person that you are genuinely interested in the insignificant details that comprise your loved one's day since it's these insignificant moments that contribute towards the reality.

Through these seeming nondescript questions, you are demonstrating your interest in their interests. You are showing them that you care enough about them to show interest in the smallest details concerning their life. These can be relationship clinchers.

4. Listen mindfully.

You can only tune in to insignificant everyday details when you actively listen to your partner. The knowledge that you are heard and understood (or lack of it) in a relationship can without exaggeration make or break it. When you know you are heard and understood, it cements your connection with the other. Practice active listening where you do not just listen keenly to what the person is saying but also acknowledges and understand it.

Understanding or recognition of the other person's emotional experiences or insignificant details can be conveyed in multiple ways including a verbal acknowledgment (such as I understand), smile, and so on.

Active listening may also involve interrupting the speaker for clarifications or confirming understanding through paraphrasing. Ask your partner or loved one for permission before interrupting him/her. Say something such as, "Sorry Jane, can I quickly ask you something?" Then pose your question in a manner that signifies that you are attempting to clarify what your partner has just said. If you disagree or want to chip in with your two cents, wait until they've finished speaking. Express disagreement only after the person has finished talking. If you aren't sure what the person said, ask for further clarifications without disagreeing aggressively or lying. Ask questions without assuming the answers.

5. Talk about yourself too.

When I tell people that the basis for a solid and long-lasting relationship is to practice active listening for acknowledging and understanding your partner's emotions, they often get into ninja listening mode. Talking doesn't have to be sacrificed at the altar of listening though. Maintain a healthy balance where both you and your loved one or partner have an equal opportunity to participate in talking and listening. Identify a healthy balance between speaking and listening since this is the most challenging aspect of any relationship. Both the partners should get a chance to express their feelings and hear/understand the other person's feelings.

What Is Emotional Connection?

Emotional connection is nothing but the attunement couples in interpersonal relationships have towards each other's emotions or feelings. Every time we identify that someone is meaningful to our partner, we connect emotionally by turning towards them. Each time our partner makes a bid to connect with us, and we respond positively to their bid by recognizing that something has meaning for them, we build or create an emotional connection.

Let us take an example. "I gave my first presentation today as a Sr. Manage." This can be a bit of an emotional connection. Turning towards your partner response can include something such as, "Wow, tell me about it. How was it? I am sure people must've loved you." A turning away response can include something such as, "hmmm, okay." Then there is a turning against response that can be downright negative. In this case, it can be something such as, "Alright, whatever! Please allow me to work undisturbed now."

On the whole, women make more bids for connection over men. Men typically make an attempt to send out these connection bids when they perceive a threat to the relationship. On the other hand, women are more inclined to make them periodically, irrespective of the health of a relationship. Men aim to turn things around by sending out these emotions bids, while women aim to nurture and maintain the relationship by regularly sending out emotional bids. Missing an emotional bid is the mental counterpart of physically turning away from a person while he/she is talking to us. The most challenging part where emotional bids are concerned is that 80 percent of people don't even attempt to make them or get them right. At times, emotional bids are concealed in form of criticism, argument, grudges, and complaints.

Turning away can primarily happen due to lack of emotional sensitivity, apathy, or the partner in engaged in repressed negativity such as passive aggressiveness or stonewalling. When you lack emotional sensitivity, you miss opportunities to turn towards your partner. One of the major causes of infidelity in relationships is lack of emotional connection. When partners miss responding to other person's emotional bids or turn away from it, they send/compel them to look elsewhere for an emotional connection.

Chapter 4:

Creating Shared Meaning to Boost Your Relationship

We all get into a relationship filled with hopes, desires, and dreams of what the interpersonal relationship has in store for us. It is these desires, visions, and hopes along with the shared meaning we build from them that bolsters our relationship, keeping it alive and kicking in times of challenges and conflicts. This chapter explains the importance of developing shared meaning in the relationship since a shared vision minimizes conflict and prevents the bond from becoming dysfunctional. We will explore how shared meaning can be the foundation of success in intimate relationships. I I'll also equip you with a bunch of actionable strategies for building a shared vision with your partner for enjoying a rewarding, lasting, and fulfilling relationship.

As per the Gottman Institute, the happiest relationships are marked by shared meaning between the couple. When we get into a relationship, we are two separate entities — two distinct, independent entities with visions, goals, desires, interests, preferences, aspirations and dreams of our own. When the relationship materializes, the two entities create a third entity, which is the relationship. When we treat the relationship as an entity and realize that it needs energy, thought, and effort to be nurtured and sustained, we can create shared meaning within the relationship.

This means identifying and including the dreams, aspirations, and hopes of both partners. It also goes beyond these to create something bigger that is a reflection of the relationship. The novel entity has emerged from the combined dreams and visions. This way, the relationship builds its own unique identity along with a shared life. Relationships that are marked by a purposeful shared meaning, objective, and values retain its charm, energy, and vibrancy. They can rough out the challenges of conflict, and are not likely to be locked into everyday problems.

Making daily or weekly togetherness rituals enables you to not just spend more quality time with your significant other but also strengthen your bond as a couple over shared experiences and rituals. Consciously create a ritual for spending time together so you don't slip into a mode where the relationship is simply 'passing the night' and not thriving. Focus on investing more time together in small yet enjoyable activities that bring shared pleasure to both you and your partner.

Establishing your own independent culture that is unique and relevant to the partnership, where you create your own ritual, customs, traditions, and myths, help maintain a strong connection in the long run. Regular connection rituals are integral to the creation of shared meaning that can, for example, include a special way of greeting each other after getting home from work or using special endearing terms for each other (addressing or calling your significant other using special terms). Then there are rituals such as uncorking a champagne bottle on special occasions. There can be stories you share as a couple about the relationship, which also creates shared meaning.

There can be a myth of how the couple met, a story behind how they fell in love, events related to a disastrous honeymoon, and a funny 'meet the parents' incident. These stories, memories, and experiences all combine to create a space that includes their dreams, hopes, and aspirations, which keeps evolving as the relationship grows and develops. These rituals and customs breed intimacy and build a commonly shared meaning along with the space to articulate this meaning.

What is shared meaning? Shared meaning is creating a common culture that only the two people in the relationship are aware of or share. What contributes to a common culture in a relationship?

Here are a few examples.

Few insider jokes, daily habits, symbols and rituals, funny memories, couple secrets, references, anniversaries, foods, visions and more. It is all this and even all the things that we don't talk about. For instance, as a couple, you may enjoy catching a movie together late into the night on weekends. You may not speak about this. However, constantly doing it makes it a part of your shared meaning and couple culture. If both you and your partner enjoying boisterous partying instead of reading books, that's also part of the shared culture.

Couples who create shared meaning are likelier to build intimacy. In a sense, shared meaning becomes the glue that keeps couples together for long.

Here are some ways to create shared meaning for strengthening your bond.

1. Have a common vision

One of the best ways to create deeper shared meaning within an interpersonal relationship is to have a common dream, objective, or vision in life with your partner. It can be anything from traveling the world to opening a dance school to starting an NGO for the underprivileged. Having a shared goal, vision, or dream brings you closer to your partner while helping you both bond over shared ideas and experiences. The entire process of fulfilling the vision can bring you both together, and help you both garner a healthy shared perspective. When couples have common dreams and visions, the unavoidable highs and lows of the relationships become less significant! They are firmly fixated on the bigger picture and are capable of overlooking the smaller, insignificant differences.

Keep a larger context of meaning for the relationship to avoid concentrating on the smaller, niggling everyday stuff. Talking about a shared vision can strengthen attunement. Take time to understand and calibrate your dreams and visions to strengthen the relationship or bring you closer to your significant other. An important objective is to create an environment that encourages both the partners to talk and air their dreams and convictions in a genuine way. If a person doesn't feel comfortable sharing his/her convictions, visions, passions and goals with his/her partner, they are less likely to bond over shared meaning. Couples who speak about their dreams, visions, and hopes with each other openly are likelier to stay happy together and less likely to struggle.

Implementing or fulfilling shared goals as a couple can lend a greater purpose to the relationship. For example, your shared goals as a couple may involve volunteering for the community, adopting a minimalist lifestyle, building more sustainable living practices, and raising your children together in a particular manner.

Healthy relationships aren't so much about having similar personalities as they are about having shared visions and goals. Build an open communication channel for airing your dreams, visions, and life purpose. Similarly, become excited by or share the other person's dreams, objectives, and visions too. Few things mar a relationship than a different life purpose or vision. Irrespective of what this shared vision, life purpose or goal is, it has the power to strengthen your relationship.

You can intentionally and purposefully build a shared vision as a couple to strengthen your bond. This allows you to prioritize your time and energy towards things that can lend more meaning to the relationship. Think about it as your own special shared couple legacy where there will be plenty of stories, shared experiences, cultural memories, etc. that can be narrated to people together. This shared meaning system has the potential to become a couple's shared legacy.

To create a stronger and more meaningful relationship, couples need to foster attunement. Talking about a shared vision leads to greater attunement or connection at a psychological level. Take time to identify, process, and understand each other's dreams/vision to come closer. Couples who consistently practice emotional attunement and turn towards each other rather than away from each other are less likely to end their marriage. A shared vision can literally be a relationship saver even though it may not appear huge on the face of it.

It is not like couples who turn towards each other do not have disagreements or challenges in their relationship. They have their share of relationship troubles too. However, when they disagree, they are still able to keep the connection and engagement alive. Unlike 'turn away' couples, they don't become hurtful, disrespectful, and defensive during disagreements. Even their arguments and disagreements are laced with affection, mutual respect, a healthy regard for each other's feelings and interest. They are able to keep their fights clean and non-hurtful because they've built a solid deposit of emotional connections (remember the analogy we discussed in an earlier chapter?). They are able to dip into the reserves of their emotional connections (built through shared visions and rituals) to overlook temporary differences and disagreements.

Building shared meaning is about defining your couple legacy. It can begin with personal exploration about the twosome's life mission, purpose, dreams and more you are trying to accomplish. Take a while to write notes related to personal legacy. When you've both gathered your thoughts, find time to share and explore them together as a couple.

Note that this becomes even more powerful when as a couple, you've laid the foundation for building a strong friendship and handling differences/conflict. It needs creativity, expressiveness, and courage to talk about your innermost dreams. When you reveal your innermost dreams to your partner, it reveals that you want to share a part of your inner self with them. As a couple, provide a safe haven for each other. Building intentional and purposeful agreement is the basis of creating shared meaning.

2. Make a list of daily and weekly shared meaning rituals to boost connections.

Make an effort to spend time doing pleasurable and enjoyable activities together. Couples should commit to creating small and meaningful rituals around the schedule such as saying goodbye in a particular manner while leaving home in the morning and end of the day reunions.

Our rituals help us along the long route of our relationship. It can be daily, weekly, or annual rituals that help us establish these small and meaningful connections in small yet significant ways. It is suggested that we begin and end every day with a ritual to strengthen our togetherness. So, you can begin by exercising together or practicing yoga/meditation each morning and end the day by watching your favorite television series by snuggling up in bed. Then, there can be weekly rituals like meeting for lunch or coffee in the middle of a workday or taking a hiking trip together every Saturday.

On a psychological level, it habituates your emotional connection or bond and teaches you both into a strong and lasting relationship. Apart from rituals, newly married and pre-married couples also have the chance of exploring objectives, visions, symbols, and roles collectively. It can start with something as basic as a conversation about the connotations of the terms, "husband" and "wife" for both.

You can pose each other questions such as:

- What do these roles imply to you?
- What did they mean in your household when you were growing up?
- What are the expectations and assumptions you have from these roles?

You can have similar conversations about other roles to understand what you and your partner associate with each role. For example, what does it mean to be a parent, friend, daughter/son, daughter-in-law/son-in-law, sibling, and so on? Similarly, when it comes to goals, objectives, and symbols, what do home, money, job, sex, and leisure mean? You'll get an opportunity to discover shared visions and goals, and determine if you and your partner are on the same page where major roles, visions, outlooks, and ideas are concerned. This can help you establish strong emotional connections based on shared visions and ideas.

Notice how every word I've mentioned above symbolizes a broader idea or concept. It is an intangible idea that these represented by these seeming tangible words. You can dive deeper into your partner's views about the intangible concepts with the help of these tangible words. For example, money could symbolize success, power, freedom, fulfilling dreams and more to some people. What are a person's goals related to these concepts? You can find out only when you have a conversation with your partner about it.

For example, let us look at a word such as intimate. No one has established for sure what the word suggests. It has different interpretations and connotations for different people. While one partner may interpret intimacy as sexual intimacy, the other may view it as emotional closeness. There is a conspicuous disconnect here between the two partners on the conceptual interpretations of intimacy. What if one partner says, "I don't think we share healthy intimacy levels" (where they may be referring to emotional intimacy), while the other partner interprets this as "we should have sex more often."

There is some disconnect there because the couple doesn't have a shared meaning or understanding of the concept of intimacy. Wouldn't it be easier if they had discussed the connotations of intimacy together and created a shared meaning that combined emotional and physical intimacy? We can't relate to our partner if we speak different languages where important concepts are concerned. Only when we discuss the implications of these terms with each other are we able to arrive at a shared connotation for crucial concepts that concern us as a couple.

Building a shared meaning can be the most fulfilling and gratifying aspects of a relationship. It makes you feel one or aligned with your partner, thus helping you both tide through the most challenging phases in the relationship. When you begin a relationship by ensuring that there is shared meaning (not that it cannot be built later), both the partners can save themselves plenty of pain down the line.

Build rituals that belong to you and your partner exclusively. In a majority of times, we connect rituals with holidays and it isn't always possible to exclude other family members and friends from holidays and festivals such as Christmas and Thanksgiving. However, building rituals into your daily and weekly interactions as a couple reinforces your commitment to each other and the relationship. It reinforces your desire to keep the spark in your relationship alive.

Commit to at least 4-6 magic hours a week as a couple where you spend time enjoying your exclusive couple rituals and where no one else but you both are involved. This can include special partings before leaving for work, spending dedicated time complimenting or appreciating each other, demonstrating affection for one another in several forms, and taking the time to narrate stories or ask questions. It can also be time to tackle elephants in the room or tricky issues that you've wanted to address since long. Devote special time for this in addition to daily rituals such as making it a point to have breakfast or dinner together. How about a stress reduction routine at the end of the day? Or maybe going to bed at one time instead of watching television or playing games on the phone? Then, you can create some weekend rituals. Maybe have a cup of coffee and breakfast out every Saturday morning before the children are up. How about working out together to stay fit as a couple?

Creating shared meaning as a couple doesn't have to be tough or grand. It can be a once in a lifetime experience that you share as a couple. Maybe a cruise trip that you can talk about for the rest of your life. Then there are annual, weekly, and daily rituals woven into your daily schedule. I have friends who color co-coordinate their outfits according to the day of the week. They'll both wear a particular color that symbolizes how they feel on each day of the week. They've been doing this for the last two decades, and it works wonderfully well for both. It may look weird to others, but it's something that works for them as a couple. It is totally their thing.

Start creating your shared meaning together as a couple right away. Begin by expressing a dream or formulating a plan, however simple it sounds. Stick to this plan no matter what. Create and pursue a common goal, which is an incredible way to build commitment, affection, and trust. These turn out to be the foundation of any relationship and have the power to withstand bonds in the face of challenges and struggles.

3. Have fun together.

In the book *Fighting for Your Marriage,* author Harold J. Markman, Ph.D., mentioned that the amount of enjoyment, pleasure, and fun couples have as partners help nurture and strengthen their connection. It is an important factor when it comes to predicting the overall success of a relationship. Though couples in the initial stages of their relationship are capable of having a lot of fun, it fizzles out with time.

New relationships are exciting, pleasurable, fun and stimulating. However, it is building a deeper and meaningful ritual around these initially fun rituals that strengthen a couple's bond over a longer period.

Thus, you can continue the rituals you enjoyed together as a couple during your dating and courtship days even after marriage to keep the shared moments, experiences and fun sparks alive. I know a couple who made a pact of enjoying the same rituals that they did during their courtship phase even after getting married and becoming parents. They diligently took time out from their responsibilities and commitments to repeat the rituals they enjoyed together as a couple. Needless to say, they are still going strong after three children and a hectic professional life.

What did they do differently from the average couple? They were committed to creating more shared meaning and experiences in their married life to keep the spark alive, something that most couples in long-term relationships take for granted. They were committed to doing more fun and exciting things long after the initial 'love rush' was over to make the relationship more meaningful in the long run. Fun and stimulation of the earlier stages can quickly fade away when the relationship is marked by routine and responsibilities. However, by developing and nurturing shared meaning over a longer haul, you will experience a deeper connection. This results in a positive overall effect on the relationship.

Couples who make the time and effort to create shared meaning and objectives are far likelier to cultivate a strong sense of intimacy which is the basis of lasting and matured relationships. Intimacy is not something that happens by chance. Often, couples try to take the quick-fix and wait for some secret force or attraction to determine their chemistry. Much as an 'instant connection' is a highly romanticized idea, intimacy doesn't happen by chance. It is a deliberately nurtured factor that has the power to sustain interpersonal relationships even in the midst of challenges.

Bear in mind that nurturing a deeper connection with your partner doesn't imply that you put them on a pedestal or that the relationship is completely devoid of any differences/problems. Intimacy isn't about sidestepping challenges, differences or conflicts. It is about disagreeing with the other person in a healthy manner and respecting the other person's right to disagree. There will be conflicts and disagreements in any normal relationship.

However, if you build a strong bank of shared meaning, these differences will be insignificant and inconsequential when compared to the bigger goals and vision. A healthy relationship isn't defined as one where there are no differences. It is, in fact, one where there is a clear coping mechanism in place to overcome these differences. And one of the most powerful coping mechanisms is shared meaning or experiences.

Overall, if you respect and adore your partner, you will conduct yourself in a manner that will overlook small differences in view of the deeper, stronger, and more meaningful connection. Even when couples don't see eye to eye on every aspect, shared goals align them, and keep them together.

If you have to overcome challenges in the relationship, weave quality time into your daily and weekly schedule to consistently recall and verbalize constructive dreams shared by you and your partner.

4. Cultural artifacts.

Pick cultural artifacts that have meaning for the both of you and make it a shared symbol or sign for your relationship. Let it represent everything your relationship stands for. For instance, you and your partner may relish Italian food after living in Italy for long. Thus, Italian food becomes a symbol of your relationship. Cultural artifacts can be anything from cities, television series, songs, and movies. These symbols can be established since your dating days.

5. Begin doing joint activities.

Sign-up for joint activities that you can do together as a couple. It can be taking the children together to the games to volunteering to backpacking to taking up a sport together.

Have you created things as a couple? You may enjoy rock-climbing together or relish Taco Tuesday. Maybe your couple thing is a shared value such as generosity or hosting guests. It can be adventure sports or working on forming an NGO. These things help you establish, set, and define your couple identity. It is how you are known as or recognized as a couple, apart from how you perceive yourself as a couple. Your partner adds value to your life, while you, in turn, add to theirs. This creates a new third and distinct entity for the relationship. By adding value to the relationship, both you and your partner make each other and third entity or relationship better.

Determining and discovering what you can do together can be a highly creative process. Begin by creating your bucket list together as a couple. Put down everything you desire to experience as a couple. What are the things you wish to learn, explore, and discover before you perish? Even if you don't think you have anything in common with the person, you'll be surprised at how much you share simply by articulating your desires and focusing on a common objective. Begin with similarities and work your way up to establish a common goal.

This way, you are able to overcome conflict in the relationship by focusing on a common goal.

6. Some marriage counselors and therapists suggest writing values.

The two partners can create rules and values for the marriage. This may not be agreeable to some couples since this can be constrictive for them. Rather than committing anything in writing, let shared meaning grow and develop over a period of time. Shared meaning should be more constructive than restrictive.

Summarizing the secrets of boosting shared meaning between your partner and you, it is safe to say that it involves spending quality time together consistently and knowing/understanding your significant half better by sharing your deepest thoughts, feelings, emotions, desires, and aspirations, which is a continuous process that takes commitment.

Chapter 5:

Conflict Resolution in Relationships

All relationships go through their share of disagreements and differences. However, the health of a relationship is determined by how both the partners deal with the disagreement.

Arguments and disagreements aren't necessarily a negative sign. It means disagreements are surfacing but they aren't been addressed. This can be owing to one partner dominating over a subservient one or because both haven't merged or know themselves well or they are giving themselves up to please each other. Not addressing arguments and differences at the right time can backfire because it builds resentment along with passive-aggressive behavior, thus killing intimacy and emotional closeness. Prevent your conflicts from escalating into power struggles and aggressive communication.

I was at a large family gathering once when I saw a glaring example of conflict resolution between an elderly couple. They were seated opposite me during dinner when the wife accidentally knocked a drink from the table on her husband who was seated next to her. As she rushed to grab some napkins, he announced, "She been following this ritual diligently for the last twenty-five years!" As the wife cleaned the spill off her husband, she laughed and turned to everyone mockingly saying, "He truly deserves it and more." Everyone laughed. The couple laughed too. Those people are known as martial masters. The make squabbles look fun and enjoyable. It isn't that they don't have a disagreement or get disagreement. However, they are still able to stay emotionally connected, cheerful, and engaged with one another. Rather than getting defensive, aggressive, or hurtful, they sprinkle their arguments with flashes of interest, affection, and respect built over emotional connections and shared meaning.

Here are some tips to keep your disagreements and arguments clean.

1. Maintain a calm, composed, and respectful stance during heated discussions.

One of the worst things people can do during heated conversations is maintaining a harsh and aggressive demeanor. Avoid crossing the line and insulting your partner. Instead, use an approach that validates and recognizes them in a calm, composed, and respectful manner. Insults and name-calling do not help validate your partner.

Instead, put your point across in a more positive and constructive manner by balancing statements. For example, it upsets me that I can't spend more time with you because it is fun being with you. You are validating your partner by stating that they are fun to be around with instead of accusing them of being selfish in not spending enough time with you. Avoid personal attacks, put-downs, and cursing. Avoid attempts to intimidate your partner or make him/her feel uncomfortable. Neither of the partners should feel attacked or threatened.

In a positive and constructive conflict, both partners are able to verbalize their needs, desires, and wants in a mutually healthy manner that breeds a solution or compromise. You reveal your intent to resolve the differences by validating and acknowledging your partner's concerns. Remember, it isn't a war that to be won. You may end up winning the argument or disagreements. However, the relationship may suffer because your partner ends up feeling deflated and resentful.

2. Get to the root of the issue.

At times, small fights, arguments, and disagreements are signs of a deeper repressed issue. Instead of sweeping the real issue under the carpet and attempting to resolve the niggling smaller fights, address the root cause of these differences. Are there any needs that are not being met? Are you placing yourself in the other person's shoes to understand things from their perspective? Avoid sweating on the smaller stuff and evaluate the larger issue.

For example, you may be upset with your partner because they are always partying with their friends, which is why you keep picking on them for every little thing. The real issue is you don't think they are giving you enough time. Evaluate things from the other person's point of view. Maybe, they are stressed after a hard day's work or desire to unwind after a hard day's work. Be understanding from the other person's perspective instead of pushing your objectives. How would things play out for you if roles were reversed?

This is related to the exploration phase. Don't attempt to sell your viewpoint to your spouse. Talk about underlying problems that contribute to the issue you are attempting to resolve. Listen mindfully to your significant half's concerns with an open and flexible mind. Learn everything about yours as well as your partner's issues. Keep your eyes on the bigger picture and form a mental list of concerns.

3. Pick your battles.

Pick your battles and agree to disagree. As a couple, you'll have to determine if what you are fighting over is worth it. Is fighting over what to have for dinner worth it? How about what movie to watch next?

Sometimes, it is best to drop these smaller issues in view of the larger picture. This is when shared meaning, emotional connections, and connection bids can come to the rescue. Even when you don't agree on the smaller things, these bigger shared memories and meaning, along with the number of times you've managed to turn in towards each other's connection bids, prove valuable. As a couple, you are guaranteed not to agree with everything. However, the overall compatibility, respect, and health of the relationship (based on the validations and acceptance you've shown each other earlier) depend on how you manage to overcome these differences.

4. Identify a middle ground.

Finding a balance or middle ground between what both you and your partner seek are critical to the health of a relationship. If both partners are concerned about making the relationship work, you will consciously work towards an agreement. Finding a middle ground is much easier than we think.

For example, if you are arguing about spending time with you and your partner's friends, you can work out an arrangement where you dedicate specific days to spend time with both or you can have days where each of you can spend time with their respective group. If you want to make things work, you will find a way. Similarly, if you feel your partner is spending more time with friends, work out an arrangement where you get to spend time with them, and they can spend time independently with their friends too.

5. Limit yourself to a single hurt.

Limit yourself to a single issue at a time. When you are disagreeing or arguing about an issue, don't keep on jumping to multiple issues. Stick to the issue at hand, and avoid fighting over anything else. For instance, "When you publically told me in the presence of our friends in a tone I believed was scornful that I was being a fool for enjoying a film you thought was terribly shallow, I felt humiliated, as though people there saw me as someone who could be mocked by her partner publically."

Limiting yourself to a single hurt helps the other person empathize with your feelings more effectively while validating the meaning assigned to the situation whether the person was feeling demeaned, disrespected, ignored or not acknowledged. Throwing a bunch of accusations about multiple feelings violated makes the person feel like they are being attacked. The focus shifts away from the issue to the person. It becomes more of a personal attack than an issue that needs resolution. Focus on tackling one issue at a time instead of going after multiple grudges. This makes the person more receptive to your feelings and emotions.

If you talk about too many issues at a time, there are lower chances of any of them being resolved. In fact, it makes the person even more defensive. The issue is pushed on the backburner, and the person assumes center stage.

6. Check with your partner whether your response led them to believe that you completely understood why they were hurt.

Inquire with your partner if your response satisfactorily convinced them that you understand why they were hurt in the first place. Consider that you've repeated what was said to you. However, only repeating what they've said to you isn't enough. You need to help them realize that you've understood them by restating what they said in your own words. Make a conscious effort to recreate what they said in your own words to confirm your understanding. Try to reframe what they said using your own verbal and non-verbal signals. Once the other person feels understood, they are likelier to calm down.

Ask yourself how it feels to be discounted and disrespected by not being heard or understood. Only when your partner is convinced that you've heard them and appreciate their feelings will they believe that a similar situation won't occur in future. If they aren't convinced that you've understood or appreciated their feelings, there will still be doubts in the mind, which will lead to further arguments in the future.

They will feel secure and safe to reveal their vulnerable side to you all over again, which is important for the intimacy of any relationship. When an individual can expand their awareness and sensitivity towards the other person's emotional suffering, there are lower chances of them repeating the hurtful behavior.

Irrespective of how misunderstood you feel, you still have to consider the other person's feelings and emotions if you want a resolution for the differences. Don't spend time or focus on explaining yourself or justifying your actions. An absolute no-no would be to interrupt them and throwing your counter-hurt. It isn't mandatory that you agree with your partner's view of reality to resolve the conflict. However, you must understand it, acknowledge it, and be sympathetic to it. It is important to validate your partner's feelings even when you disagree with them.

7. Don't build a hurt museum.

Don't build a hurt museum over a period of time. It can destroy the basis of a relationship if the relationship doesn't have enough emotional connections and shared memories to fall back on.

Our hurt comprises everything from memories of the past to our partner's hurtful comments to their disappointment. Focus on building shared memories than a hurt museum. Don't keep memories negatively charged in your mind for long. At a subterranean level, these problems continue to breed. If they fester for long, it is guaranteed that they will interfere with conflict resolution. The reason these instances resurface is that you and your partner haven't attended to this hurt or the motions. Consider if the feelings connected to every emotion is linked to feeling disregarded, dismissed, guilty, falsely blamed, victimized, manipulated, ridiculed, unimportant, devalued, powerless, humiliated, shamed, rejected, spurned, unloved, and so on.

8. Don't hesitate to enlist external help.

At times, a neutral third-party resolution is all you need to resolve a disagreement or issue. Mediators exist precisely for this objective. Mediators are professionally trained to resolve disputes between couples and using a professional mediator can lead to a cleaner, faster, and healthier resolution that can be acceptable to both the parties.

When both parties are stuck to their respective perspectives, it helps to gain a more balanced third person view. A mediator ensures that every side is given a fair chance and none of the parties leave feeling ripped off.

9. Don't get defensive when criticized.

When your partner criticizes you, defensiveness doesn't resolve issues. Visualize a couple arguing because the wife wants her husband to contribute more towards household chores. When she talks about him doing small chores after he gets ready to go for work in the morning, he says, "Yes that can be helpful but I am usually pretty busy in the mornings during rush hour."

Then, when the wife suggests he spend time completing household chores during the weekends, again he says something such as, "Yes, that can be scheduled in, but we always have plans during the weekend. At times, I also have to catch up on work. So I don't see this working." This 'yes-but' behavior suggests that the wife's ideas and views are not worth it. They are neither acknowledged nor validated. Another negative and destructive behavior can be cross-complaining. When you respond to one complaint with another, it is called cross-complaining. For example, responding to "You don't keep the house clean" with "You are obsessed with neatness." It is important to consider the other person's perspective.

Another thing that is an absolute no-no where couple arguments and disagreements are concerned, is contempt. Gottman has discovered that the single largest divorce predictor is contemptuous remarks that belittle and demean your partner. This can involve everything from name-calling to negative labeling to sarcasm. It can also encompass eye-rolling, smirking, and other disrespectful behavior. It implies disgust.

Visualize one partner saying something such as "I wish we go out more often", while the response is "Yes, the most critical thing for you is to spend time and money on overpriced food at a rip-off eatery." It couldn't get more superficial than that, could it? If one partner says something such as "I am sure you are exhausted after a long day of chatting up your co-workers and gossiping about your boss at the cooler. I work my butt off all day and you walk into the home, spread yourself on the couch, and stare at your phone like a teenager gone awry." This is the kind of contemptuous talk you should steer clear from. This makes it impossible to undertake any real discussion and evokes anger from your partner rather than resolve the issue at hand.

10. Stay away from negativity.

It can be challenging to avoid responding to a partner's bad behavior with greater bad behavior. Indulging the urge only makes the challenging situation even worse. Relationship expert Gottman and co-workers call it "negative affect reciprocity." They exchange heated insults with even more contemptuous remarks. As the conflict rages, the negativity increases. In his study, Gottman discovered that the magic figure is a 5 to 1 ratio. Couples that kept a ratio of five positive behaviors or attempts at well-meaning humor, warmth, and collaboration to every negative behavior were significantly likelier to be separated or divorced after four years.

11. Know when it is time for a timeout.

If you view yourself slipping into a negative pattern and find that either you or your partner are not following the above-mentioned strategies, take time out from the argument. Taking a short break with a few deep breaths can be enough to calm tempers. Research on arguments reveals that both controlling anger and taking the other person's perspective are important when it comes to managing conflicts effectively!

Conclusion

Thank you for reading or listening to this book.

I genuinely hope it has offered you multiple strategies about communicating with your spouse to lay the foundation of a lasting, happy, and fulfilling marriage.

How should you talk to your spouse in a manner that they listen? How should you resolve issues and get over your differences to live a more harmonious life?

The objective of the book is to help you set the tone of a long-lasting, happy, and fulfilling marriage where both the spouses have communicated each other's needs, expectations, and wishes. Communication is the key to building a solid, rewarding, and lasting marriage.

The next step is to start using the strategies mentioned in the book immediately. Begin communicating with your partner in a meaningful way, do tiny things that increase the bond of communication between you and your spouse, and be committed to the pursuit of overcoming differences through establishing shared meaning, practicing validation and establishing emotional connections. If you've just had a challenging situation in the marriage, it may not improve immediately. It may be a slow process that needs more time, dedicated effort, and attention to gradually grow into a strong and indestructible bond.

Allow the relationship to blossom by contributing in your own small ways to make your spouse feel special. Chalk out an arrangement beforehand about tackling conflicts and disagreements. Listen and think about the other person while attempting to resolve differences. Keep an open communication and objective mindset approach.

Effective Communication

Skills and Strategies to Effectively Speak Your Mind Without Being Misunderstood

Keith Coleman

Introduction

Imagine a scenario where two people who possess the equal technical knowledge, experience and skills are applying for the same job. Everything else being the same, one is a fantastic communicator who knows how to put across his/her point effectively and send out a clear, compelling and confident message. The other candidate, however, struggles to convey his/her thoughts, ideas and words. Who do you think will eventually bag the coveted job? Of course, the person possessing sound communication skills!

Communication skills act as the basis of all our relationships—personal and professional. You need it for everything from acing your job interview to pursuing the hot new date everyone is vying for. It is an essential tool for productivity, making a positive impression and professional growth. Imagine having a head full of ideas but not having the ability to express or convey these ideas. Wouldn't that be highly unfortunate? Communication gives you the power to put across your ideas assuredly and compellingly.

All our relationships in this world are determined by how we relate to people. We can't fulfill all our needs ourselves. Relating to and seeking help from other people requires communication. Do you want to see what insufficient communication can do? Well, grab a ticket, hop on a plane and fly to a destination whose language you don't have a clue about. Expressing every little detail will become a herculean task. You will have trouble finding even necessary things like food and shelter.

Communication is the ability to collaborate, shares idea with and relate to the world around you. It makes transferring ideas less challenging. The real superpower of a human is the ability to socialize, express opinions and collaborate. This is precisely what led to the creation of aircraft, automobiles, highways and electrical systems. The ability to collaborate, contribute and express ideas.

Be honest, when you meet a person for the first time, how do you form an impression about them without knowing them immediately? Through their appearance and the manner in which they communicate with you, you can form an impression of them. Similarly, you can use effective communication to sweep people off their feet in the first meeting itself, while influencing them to do what you want.

Without the process of communication or the ability to communicate, we would be limited by our brain's ability to perform tasks or share ideas. The world is about ideas and selling your ideas impressively to other people, and effective communication makes that possible. You can help persuade and convince people by creating a stellar impression. How do you think salespersons who you don't even know can sell you things which you don't even need? The answer is simple—the power of communication!

Advice on How to Use the Information in This Book, or Any Book for that Matter

Knowledge is valuable only when put into action. Otherwise, it doesn't serve any purpose.

What is the best way to gain information fast in the shortest period of time? Do you merely read books or do you use books? Power is the ability to take action. If the books you read give you the ability to act, that's real power. Information is facts, data, numbers, statistics, principles, and theories. There's plenty of information everywhere on the internet.

When you have plenty of information, it becomes knowledge. Knowledge is accumulated over a period of time. Textbooks are a source of information. You read many books, give tests to assess your understanding, and then wonder why everything in your life is the same. Think about this—maybe you haven't converted information into knowledge, and <u>knowledge into experience</u>.

Experience allows you to test the knowledge you've acquired. Making mistakes will enable you to figure out whether you've learned the right knowledge. You're observing a pattern of what works and what doesn't.

<u>Don't just read books is all I want to tell you. Use books.</u> Every person's wisdom is different, it comes from their own experiences. My wisdom may not be the same as yours. Go beyond watching videos and reading books to actually take back information and implement it. Apply information shared in this and other books to know what works for you and what doesn't. You can't learn to swim by reading about how to swim.

While reading or listening through this book, take away the three most significant and actionable ideas, lessons or techniques that you can implement right away!

Chapter 1:

13 Power Packed Tips to Enhance Your Public Speaking Skills and Communicate Effectively

One of the most significant indicators of a powerful communicator is someone who can engagingly put across their point when addressing an audience. Whether you are giving a presentation to a boardroom full of people or talking to a broad audience from a podium, some valuable pointers can help you communicate more effectively when it comes to driving home important points. Are you able to persuade and convince people of your idea? Are you able to express yourself compellingly on a public platform? Are you able to communicate with a group of people without any space for misunderstanding?

Here are 15 power packed tips to transform into a highly effective and articulate public speaker.

1. Grab Attention with a Powerful Beginning and End

This doesn't go on to say everything in between should be mediocre. It just means your beginning should be powerful enough to get your audience hooked and listening intently to the rest of the speech. Don't begin with some nondescript and uninspiring like "Today I am going to talk about so and so." It is plain, insipid and boring, and doesn't encourage your audience to listen any further.

Instead, begin with a shocking or unexpected statistic, an incredible statement, an interesting anecdote or a powerful quotation. The idea is to induce shock and interest to grab your audience's attention. Don't make it unnecessarily scandalous though, just include an element of surprise.

Similarly, while concluding the speech, offer a summary of all the important points made during the speech to reinforce what you've said, eliminating any misunderstandings. Also, close with a powerful statement or quotation that your audience is likely to remember for long. Make it unique and memorable!

2. Work with a Script but Don't Read Looking at It

I always recommend creating a rough skeleton of what you plan to say in the speech. It can include important points you wish to address or quotations/anecdotes you want to use during the speech. We are human, and there is a tendency to forget things. Work with a rough script or draft and keep building upon it as you speak. This will invariably come when you go with the flow of the speech and gauge audience reaction.

However, don't ever read from a script. Use it only as a prompt. One of the most powerful ways of connecting with your audience involves looking them in the eye and speaking. You will come across as more credible and drive home the point more effectively. If you need to look into the paper for clues, simply glance at it and then convey it to your audience by looking them in the eye. Never ever read verbatim from your notes. It makes you come across as a highly ineffective communicator.

By maintaining eye contact with your audience, you focus on the message. Create a brief and rough outline to keep on track with the speech but always communicate by maintaining eye contact with your audience. The speakers who read directly from a script make themselves appear highly ineffectual. There is no eye contact, and as a speaker, you don't come across as passionate in the points you are making. You won't light up your audience or lead them to action. It goes without saying that you need a powerful opening and closing and should have these points prepared. However, you also need to speak from your heart.

Instead of utilizing a verbatim script, use index cards for preparing your speech. Write a few words or a brief phrase on the cards to offer clues about the main idea, concept or story that you can speak about confidently.

3. Personalize and Humanize the Message

I am not lying here. I literally sleep through speeches that are clinical, staccato-like and boring. Unless your audience is a bunch of machines, avoid making your speech mechanical. As a presenter, you'll get plenty of brownie points for personalizing the message. Irrespective of the topic, there's always a way to personalize and humanize a message. It's a wonderful way to get intimate and build a connection with your audience. People relate better to stories or anecdotes, experiences of other people, stories of hope and triumphs, tragedies and challenges and more.

Add a dash of humor, however serious the topic, to make it more appealing for your audience. Stories and real-life incidents will add an element of credibility to keep your listeners hooked. Share personal views and opinions to make it more human, while avoiding controversial statements all the same. When you state your preferences or state your opinion, you come across as more human, which allows your audience to connect with you on a deeper level. Use personal interest stories and elements throughout the speech. This technique makes it easy for the audience to warm up to the speaker.

All the same, you will conquer any feelings of nervousness and anxiety, while experiencing greater ease by connecting with your audience on a deeper level. Just like your audience warms up to you, you will warm up to them. Any lingering nervousness will be overcome when you make the speech more personal. Focus on building a relationship with your audience.

4. Strengthen Your Vocal Delivery

Your voice is your power. Use it to your advantage by throwing it in the most effective manner. Your voice is one of the most flexible tools when it comes to communicating with your audience in a compelling and effective way. You can add plenty of effects, coloration, and emotions to the voice by modulating it to express the right emotions and feelings. Don't speak in a monotone or single flat tone. Use plenty of variation to make your speech more varied. It adds more punch to the speech.

For example, when you want to make a powerful statement, start on a flat note. Later, raise your pitch, and end on a flat note all over again. Don't stop on a high pitch since that makes your statement appear more like a question. End on a flat note, so it seems like you are making a powerful statement rather than a question. You can work with a speech coach if you want to make your presentation skills even more power-packed.

5. Body Language

Your body is a potent communication tool that helps convey what you are trying to say by adding more depth to your message. Through your physical expression, you will put across your point even more convincingly to the audience. What do you think are an actor's secrets of commanding the stage or leading the audience to believe something that they want them to feel? The power of body language!

Use your body language to your advantage by maintaining the right power positions throughout the speech. Understand the fact that, other than what you are verbally speaking, you are also communicating with your audience on a subconscious level through non-verbal clues. There are subtle signals being sent to them through your body language, tone, voice and more. Body language is essential because it helps complement your verbal message to ensure there is no misunderstanding or that the message is conveyed more compellingly.

Always stand while delivering a speech. Your full body form should be visible to the audience if you want them to take you seriously and come across as authoritative. Your position on the podium or room, your body movements, your hand gestures—everything adds to the speech power.

Ground yourself firmly on the podium by assuming a dominant stance. Your feet should be spread at the armpit width, while the body weight should be evenly spread. Assuming this posture offers you the feeling of stability. You will appear more balanced, credible and trustworthy. Your audience will be more likely to accept your ideas when they subconsciously perceive you to be more grounded.

Your arms should be in a neutral position. When you are self-conscious while speaking, you'll do a lot of things with the arms except leaving them unnoticed at your sides. Begin with a neutral position by keeping your arms at your sides. Next, use your hands to gesticulate while speaking. It will add more punch to the message. Don't cross or lock your arms, it is a sign of physically blocking yourself from the audience or creating a barrier (more on body language in the next chapter).

Use more open body postures, which will make you come across as a transparent, open, credible and trustworthy person. Don't keep your hand anywhere near the upper body. That part of your body should be open so that there is no barrier between you and the audience.

If you are sitting and delivering a speech, sit straight and bend slightly forward. Bring your back about one third ahead on the seat, and then lean forward slightly with the upper body! You'll appear more authoritative, professional, engaging and credible when you lean ahead. Leaning back or slouching makes you uncomfortable and isn't useful when it comes to delivering the message in a convincing manner.

Your gestures should be animated and should complement the point you're trying to make. Don't use your hands excessively; use them effectively. Gestures are meant to emphasize the point you are trying to drive home more powerfully. It can be used for amplifying your message and lending it more purpose. For example, saying "you" is not enough but saying "you" and pointing to the audience makes all the difference in emphasizing or amplifying the "you."

While some speakers have the habit of randomly wandering about the podium or stage, others stride in a more purposeful manner. Move with a greater sense of purpose and mindfulness. Know that every step you take adds to your message. Before you begin speaking about a new point, take a few steps. The movement will make the audience sit up and take notice.

6. Don't Overlook Q & A

Q & A is your best opportunity to persuade your audience when putting across your point in a compelling and persuasive manner even after the presentation is done. However, there can be plenty of questions and challenges. Speakers have an opportunity during Q & A to indulge in self-depreciating humor, rephrase the presentation, and summarize the speech to ensure there is no further misunderstanding.

Allow your audience to throw questions for greater clarity. Ask questions to check your audience's level of understanding. Avoid pointing a finger in the direction of the person who has asked the question. Instead, keep your palms open or maintain an open stance to communicate your point of view to the audience effectively and compellingly. Use Q & A to keep the audience hooked to your side.

7. Avoid Confusing Topic with Purpose

To begin with, even the best speakers confuse topic and objective/purpose. If you ask them the objective of their talk, they'll say they are going to talk about so and so topic. However, that is merely their topic, not the purpose of their speech. The purpose of their presentation is what they are trying to achieve through it. Do you want to persuade the audience into thinking like you? Do you want to sell something to them? Are you trying to gauge audience preferences or interests?

Information or topic is what you are going to share, but your objective will establish a structure for sharing that information. Gaining more clarity of purpose will help you create your presentation more effectively. Each time you start preparing a rough draft for your presentation, begin with a clear objective in mind. Once your purpose or intention is established, it is easy to work around how you are going to achieve it. I always say this— if your "why" is clear, your "how" will find a way.

8. Say it Thrice

At the starting of your presentation, tell your audience what you are going to be speaking about. Then follow it up by actually making those points in your speech. Finally, towards the end of your speech, summarize all the important points you made all over again. This is one of the golden rules of speech-making— and with sufficient reason. It works wonders. It is not just easier for your listeners to keep up with details, but also more comfortable for you to focus on the highlights of your presentation.

According to a report in Business Week, a typical United States citizen has an attention span of six minutes. Break your presentation into six-minute sound pieces for it to be more effective. Make sure your visual aids have their own headlines for easy comprehension. Plant verbal flags in every six-minute sound bite with signposting instructions like, "let me highlight this concept or idea for you more effectively!" This grabs the attention of your reader towards important points.

Learn the art of using "the perfect moment" as defined by Spalding Gray. The "perfect moment" is nothing but the moment in your speech when a huge idea is suddenly made even more powerful and brilliant. You use a moving quotation or metaphor to present your idea in a new light. Some speakers also like to use allegory for pitching their idea. Approaching the idea from a different direction makes it even more power-packed. For example, you may compare your hiring with plunging for the World Series.

9. Share Something Striking and New

Effective public speakers know that an element of shock, surprise and novelty works wonders with the audience. It isn't vital to merely share useful or valuable information with your audience. It must also be new. One of the best workarounds for this is to study contrary viewpoints to the point on a topic. Think why is this person's thinking wrong or narrow or shallow. You'll get some of your best ideas using this neat little trick. Just examine contrary viewpoints and why they are lousy to come up with new ideas on the subject.

10. Identify the One Overriding Theme

Ask yourself what the overriding theme or idea of your presentation or talk is. If you had to sum it up in under 15 words, what would you say? A group of great ideas connected with the help of one, powerful and overriding theme that resonates with your audience. Don't have a ready list of desperate and haphazard ideas. They will go as soon as they appear.

Have a unifying theme that puts things into perspective for your audience. Also, if you keep a single theme, it will be tough for editing the fluff and digressing from the main point.

11. Offer a Clear Call to Action

One of the best ways to conclude what you are trying to say is to give your audience a clear call of action. People are generally lazy and don't like to think too much. The chances of them doing exactly what you want them to do increases if you tell them what to do instead of assuming that they know what to do! Finish by giving them an explicit call to action. What you've done during the speech is induced a sense of passivity in people.

They have been sitting and absorbing what you've been saying as a passive audience. Now you want to get them into action or go from being passive to active. Towards the end of the speech or presentation, it is time for them to assimilate the message more actively. This way they are more likely to remember the message, and even act upon what you are saying.

Consider this example. According to author and speech coach Nick Morgan of Power Cues: The Subtle Science of Leading Groups, Persuading Others, and Maximizing Your Personal Impact, the best call to action he's ever seen involves something he saw at a charitable event. At the end of his speech, the speaker urged everyone to reach into their pocket for loose change. He then instructed the audience to hold it out at arm's length. Once done, he instructed everyone to throw the loose change on the floor.

There were over 5000 people in the audience, and the sound was just spectacular. Runners went and collected the money. Guess what? Thousands of dollars were raised for the cause of AIDS within moments. This is exactly what a compelling call to action does—it drives people into taking action in the right direction.

12. Offer a Solution

Draft a speech that explicitly addresses the audience's problems and offers them a solution. They must have something to take back home. It is an age-old persuasion formula used wonderfully by the Greeks over 2,000 years back and still holds good. Structure a speech where you create a problem or identify an apparent problem that the audience is facing. Later, pitch your product as a solution to the issue.

You'll draw their attention to the problem or highlight their issue at the beginning of the speech by asking relevant, attention-grabbing questions. It works wonders because you take your audience through a cycle of emotions. It starts with a feeling of fear, insecurity or uncertainty when you ask questions related to their problem. Then, you make them feel better at the end of the presentation by offering a solution. This fear- relief cycle works on a psychological level to create positive feelings in your audience at the end of the speech.

When you are trying to sell an idea, concept, product or service to people, always focus on the value or benefit it has for the audience over product/service features. Features are nothing more than characteristics of the product. However, solutions are how the product or service can benefit the customer.

13. Use Humor Liberally

Sometimes to shake the audience out of their boredom and lethargy, you have to infuse some humor into the speech. It makes you come across as charming, intelligent and exciting. At times, you want to inform people without sounding dull. You want them to be informed and entertained, so the point is driven home even more effectively.

The most relatable humor comes in personal anecdotes. People who share their own experiences or have the ability to laugh at themselves come across as exceedingly charming. Everyone loves a person who is confident enough to poke fun at themselves. Think about an embarrassing moment that you may have found funny and use it in your speech.

You may have read about it somewhere or had a funny conversation with a friend about it. Incorporate it into your speech as a personal experience to make the narration funnier conversation. Take inspiration for humor from your own life, drama and everyday foibles. Be a reasonable observer to be a good humorist. Observe and absorb everything around you to find humor in it that may appeal to people or sound highly relatable.

However grim or severe the situation, you can always incorporate humor to make it more interesting, relatable and compelling. Along with fear, humor works wonderfully well when it comes to effectively putting across your point.

I would highly recommend practicing your delivery with small groups when it comes to using humor. Sometimes even a seemingly good joke or punch line may fall flat on its face if not delivered effectively. Experiment with a small focus group. If they don't find a joke or anecdote genuinely funny, you may have to rework your method of delivery.

Practice delivering punch lines more effectively before you actually say them in front of an audience. It requires a certain amount of skill, throw of voice and expressions to gain the desired reaction from your audience. Use humor that you are comfortable with. If you use quips or jokes only for the sake of sounding funny while feeling exceedingly uncomfortable while saying, it will reflect in the way you say it.

Also, you have to be comfortable stating the anecdote or joke from memory. Include enough details for the audience to form a mental image of the situation. Set up your humorous piece, and lead your audience towards the punch line. Humor must be delivered in a conversational and exciting manner. Blend it effortlessly into your speech. Don't make your story or anecdote too long-winded since people tend to lose patience. Deliver your punch line by the third or fourth line.

One of the golden rules of effective communication is a passion for a subject. Humor should flow. If you have to try too hard to make it happen, just drop it. Sometimes, even the most boring topics can be brought alive by infusing some humor.

Another little-known trick is to avoid signposting that something funny is coming up. Don't kill it by saying something like, "let me share a funny story." Allow the audience to determine if it is funny or not. Always appear pleasant and cheery, while launching into a funny story. Move through it as if you are sharing something serious. This will take away the pressure to be funny. Don't transform into a comedian within a matter of minutes. The idea is to use humor merely as a tool. Also, keep the humor related to the point you are trying to express.

Do not force it into the speech merely to appear funny. Tie it with some aspect of what you are trying to express. You may end up sidetracking what you are trying to communicate. Most importantly, you should find your piece of humor funny. If it doesn't make you laugh or bring a smile to your face, you can't communicate how funny it is to your audience.

Chapter 2:

Actionable Body Language Tips to Compliment Your Verbal Skills

Nonverbal communication contributes to about 93 percent of the communication process, with body language and tone of voice playing a huge role in putting across your point in a compelling manner or creating a stunning first impression. What distinguishes effective communicators from people who struggle to put across their point is the ability to use their body language and voice to communicate their message compellingly. When you use nonverbal communication channels in conjunction with effective verbal communication skills, there are lower chances of being misunderstood. You may speak your mind in a more confident, convincing, persuasive and compelling manner.

1. Fake Confidence with a Power Pose

Research conducted at the Harvard and Columbia Business Schools revealed that by merely holding your body in an expansive posture or occupying more space while sitting in a high power pose allows you to fake confidence. Another power pose is leaning back with your hands resting behind the head and keeping your feet on the desk. Standing with arms and legs stretched wide also works wonders when it comes to exuding confidence and power. What happens is these power poses will increase your testosterone levels and convey a subtle message of power to the subconscious mind.

Once the hormone linked to dominance, confidence, and power is activated, the brain is automatically led to believe you are powerful and confident. Thus, the subconscious mind further directs our actions in line with this thought. Confident poses lead to positive and powerful thoughts, which in turn create more of these powerful poses. These poses help you project confidence and feel more satisfied from within.

Assume high power poses during an important meeting or negotiation. Standing tall with your shoulders pulled slightly back, expanding your stance, spreading your arms to occupy more space are all known to raise the body's testosterone levels, closely linked to self-confidence, self-assuredness, and power. This effect is reversed when you assume more defensive and confidence lacking positions.

Let's take an example of you waiting in the reception area for a crucial meeting. How are you sitting or waiting for that all important meeting? Are you bending over to see your smartphone with your shoulders hunched and elbows pulled into the waist? Are you sitting upright with your feet firmly placed on the floor, and arms spread wide while reading a newspaper? When you are actually called for the negotiation or meeting, whichever of the two hormones (testosterone and cortisol) is most dominant in the body chemistry will make all the difference.

2. Remove Barriers to Inspire Collaboration

If you want to collaborate with a person or people, don't assume physically obstructive poses that are detrimental to the process. Even something as simple as holding a glass or cup of coffee between you and the potential collaborator can create a mental barrier!

The thing about non-verbal cues is they are unlike verbal cues; they are **communicated at a subconscious** level. Since primitive times, when language wasn't yet introduced, men communicated through non-verbal cues and some of these have survived throughout evolution.

When you keep a physical barrier between you and the other person, you are distancing yourself from them or blocking them out. This is the subliminal message they receive. While negotiating or cracking a business deal or merely getting someone to subscribe to your views, avoid crossing your arms and feet. Leave your feet, arms and palms open. Hold your coffee cup or glass at waist level rather than holding it higher if you want to project a more confident, open and less obstructive persona. Your face and chest should face the other person without any physical obstruction or barrier.

3. Stimulate Positive Feelings by Smiling

This is another universal expression that has been in place since the beginning of an evolution for conveying likability and good feelings. A smile doesn't just trigger your sense of well-being but also makes you come across as a more friendly, approachable and trustworthy person.

Now, there is a massive difference between faking a smile and offering a genuine smile. When you smile genuinely, the skin around your eyes crinkles. A fake smile doesn't reach the eyes. Look out for wrinkles around the eyes (crow's feet) and mouth when you want to tell if a person is offering a genuine smile.

When you smile at someone, they will likely return the smile, which will stimulate positive feelings in them. Therefore, smiling is one of the most potent ways of triggering positive feelings in people's emotions. It influences how people feel about you and puts them in a more positive and receptive state of mind. They are less likely to resist what you say when you initially establish a positive rapport.

4. Mirroring People to Build Rapport

This is a secret trick to lead people into believing that you are one among them. You are establishing a favorable rapport on a powerful subconscious level by demonstrating that you are just like them. Start by minutely observing a person's body language when they are interacting with you. What is their posture like? What are their frequently used gestures? What words and phrases do they always drop in their conversation? How are they standing or sitting? Then, subtly follow suit.

Mirror their expressions, posture, and gestures. Try to use the same words and phrases they use frequently. Your mirroring should be very subtle and inconspicuous, or it may backfire. They shouldn't get the impression that you are mocking or mimicking them. If they are holding their glass in a particular manner, follow suit. Sip on your drink soon after they sip on theirs. If they are leaning against the bar, assume the same position.

The idea is to mirror their actions to send a subconscious message that you are like them or one among them. This will come across as more trustworthy, and they'll be more receptive to your ideas and actions. The technique is so powerful because it is effective on a highly primordial level to induce feelings of belongingness, affiliation, and similarity. Men used mirroring to convey a sense of belongingness and similarity even before the invention of language. Also, when a person is mirroring your actions, he/she may be desperately seeking your validation.

5. Keep Your Voice Down to Appear Authoritative

Yes, the secret to appearing authoritative is to avoid raising your voice. Keep it steady and low to appear in control of the situation. Compelling and reliable people seldom lose control. Raising your voice by letting your emotions take over is a sign of losing control. Allow your tone to be steady and the voice, low. Watch that your voice or tone doesn't have a high inflection at the end of sentences since this suggests you are asking a question rather than making a statement.

It conveys to the other person that you are seeking their validation or approval. Your voice should maintain a flat note towards the end of a sentence to communicate more compellingly. If you want to state an opinion more authoritatively, use the power arc. Begin on a note, then raise your pitch ever so slightly through the statement, and then let it drop towards the end of the sentence. It will make you come across as more dominant when stating your opinion.

6. Improve Your Speech by Using Gestures

Brain imaging studies have revealed the brain's Broca area, vital for speech production, is highly active not just when we are speaking, but also when we gesticulate with our hands. Our hand gestures and speech is inextricably woven, which means gesturing when we speak powers up our thoughts and speech. Your verbal content will improve dramatically if you get into the habit of gesturing animatedly using your hands.

Start by practicing before the mirror. You'll soon discover that the mere act of gesturing, while also using shorter and more effective sentences, aids in clarifying your thoughts. There is a tendency to use more powerful, declarative language when you use your hands for gesticulating. Try, it works wonders!

Along with hand gestures, powerful speakers also move around throughout the room while speaking. Movement is symbolic of energy, which in turn conveys power and confidence. You come across as more expressive and animated. Avoid keeping your hands in your pockets while addressing people. It will only make you come across as a closed, intimidated and insecure individual. Always reveal your palms while speaking. The upward palm gesture makes you come across as more likable, affable and trustworthy.

7. Appear Like You Are Listening

Sadly, a majority of people fail to realize that communication is as much about listening as it is about talking. Don't appear occupied or try to multitask when someone is talking to you. Avoid checking your phone, or reading the newspaper when people are speaking to you. This lowers their level of participation. The right way is to face them, make eye contact and lean slightly forward (to communicate attention and interest). Uncross your arms and legs when they are speaking.

Keep your palms open, and shoulders held back.

Nod your head while they are speaking as a gesture of acknowledging what they are sharing. It shows you are interested or engaged in what they are saying or paying close attention. If you want people to form a favorable impression of you or desire to increase their participation, give them the impression that you are genuinely listening to them. It works wonders when it comes to establishing a favorable rapport with people. Do everything you can to ensure they know you are hearing them out. This will work wonderfully in your favor!

8. Establish Instant Connections by Shaking Hands

Touch is one of the most potent primitive cues when it comes to establishing a quick connection with people. Touching someone's shoulder or hand even for a fraction of a second evokes positive feelings and helps create an instant bond. Shaking hands is a great way to establish a connection through touch, especially when you are meeting someone for the first time.

According to research conducted by the Center for Trade Shows, people are twice as likely to recall meeting you if you've shaken hands with them. People view you as more forthcoming, affable and open when you offer a handshake. However, ensure that you get the handshake right because it can make or break your first impression. A limp handshake can be a sign of submissiveness, cowardliness, and insufficient confidence. You won't come across as an assertive and self-assured person if you offer a weak and limp handshake.

Similarly, a crushing handshake (where you are literally crushing the other person's hand) makes you come across as highly aggressive, dominating and intimidating. The handshake should neither be too limp or too aggressive, it should be firm without squashing the other person's hand. A firm handshake makes you come across as confident, self-assured and in control of the situation without appearing overbearing and intimidating.

9. Use Spacing for Effective Non-Verbal Communication

Spacing varies from culture to culture in the sense that different cultures across the world have diverse ideas about the amount of physical space to be maintained while communicating with different groups of people. However, social distancing is typically broken into distinct categories.

Intimate distance is touching the other person at 45 centimeters. It is entering an individual's intimate zone, which can be highly discomforting or unsettling for some people. Never enter a person's innermost area unless you already have a close rapport with him or her or are willingly welcomed into it by the other person.

Social distance is the normal distance generally maintained between people in social situations. These are more impersonal or professional-like interactions with an average length of 1.2 m to 3.6 m between people. Maintaining eye contact and keeping your speech loud and audible is vital while keeping a social distance from people. The next is public distance, 3.7 m to 4.7 m between two people. Some examples are teachers addressing groups of students or business boardroom presentations. Here hand and head movements gain more significance since facial expressions are not visible.

10. Increase Your Visual Dominance Ratio by Maintaining Eye Contact

If you want to increase your visual dominance ratio (ratio of who is looking into the other person's eyes while speaking and who is looking elsewhere), look into the other person's eyes! This is a sign of great confidence. Visual dominance also helps establish where you stand concerning the other person. People who look more away than into the other person's eyes are considered to possess a low social dominance factor. People who don't look away often are the boss of the situation!

Similarly, folks who look downward demonstrate helplessness and submissiveness because it seems like they are trying to avoid confrontation or conflict. If you want to up your visual dominance ratio, maintain consistent eye contact with a person. Based on the context, making eye contact can be viewed as a sign of showing respect, authority or attraction.

For instance, if you are addressing a room full of professionals via a business presentation, always direct your comments to one side of the audience and then another. Divide the audience into two or three parts and then address your comments to each section to make your presentation more power-packed. Also, get into the habit of picking out people to discuss your comments. People who are sitting around the person you are addressing will think you are having direct communication with the person, this increases your rating as an orator.

Watch out for clues that indicate engagement or insufficient engagement on the part of your audience. If a person is constantly shaking his or her head, they are seeking your approval or validation. They are keen on making a favorable impression on you or are highly concerned about the opinion you have about them. Similarly, tilting your head slightly downward or gazing elsewhere can demonstrate disengagement. Slumping on the chair is also a huge sign of disengagement or lack of interest/attention. So are writing, fidgeting and doodling.

Also, if you are trying to make an important point during a meeting, do it at the beginning of the conversation. The input is more likely to be trivialized if it saved for the end. By addressing the issue or point, however small it is, at the beginning of the meeting, you are setting yourself up as a person who is willing to participate. After addressing the main point at the beginning of the meeting, when you share your insights, recommendations, and suggestions at the end of the meeting, they are well received.

11. Pause and Movement When Making a Presentation

Human beings are intrinsically attracted to movement. When you move while speaking, people are bound to give you attention because their eyes invariably move in your direction. When you want to make an important point, move towards the audience. Space can also be used powerfully for presenting your ideas in a more compelling manner.

For instance, let us say you want to make four crucial points throughout the presentation. Speak about each of the points by assuming a distinct physical position. Again, if you are speaking about the advantages and disadvantages of something or have some good news and bad news for your audience, each of it can be presented from different sides of the stage or podium. However, ensure that your closing remarks are made from the positive or good side. Where movement is concerned, don't move when making a meaningful comment. For maximum impact, combine movement with pauses where you stand still for highlighting the most crucial points of your presentation.

12. Walk with Plenty of Energy

Imagine you are interacting with someone for the first time. They walk towards you in slow, unsure steps. Next, imagine the same person walking towards you with higher energy and purposefulness. This simple shift in the way a person is walking can help change people's impression of him or her. How you walk is a clear indicator of your confidence, self-esteem, attractiveness, and credibility.

Also, project plenty of confidence when you speak. No one will buy your words if you come across as an unsure and inhibited speaker. To inspire people's trust, you need to appear confident and self-assured while talking. If you suffer from anxiety, nervousness or fear while speaking to an audience, overcome these issues first with plenty of practice. You may need therapy too in extreme cases. Always project a powerful voice, body language and persona to appear confident. Listeners will trust you more and are likelier to do what you ask them to when they see you as a person who knows what they are saying.

13. Assume the Super Model Pose to Prevent People from Feeling Threatened

Standing face to face with a person may make them feel more threatened or confrontational. One of the best ways to avoid coming across as threatening or intimidating is to move your stance a little, so you end up standing in a position like supermodels that seldom stand with their bodies facing the camera. When you are confronted, instead of backing away, merely shift the angle slightly.

If you don't want to give the impression of being confrontational or wish to appear less intimidating, approach the individual and stand at an angle at 45 degrees, while maintaining direct eye contact with the person. Try to stand beside the person to signify collaboration over confrontation and competition.

14. Manage Facial Expressions

Whether you realize this or not, your expressions can communicate your innermost feelings subconsciously to people! Yes, they reveal more than you think. Use this knowledge to your advantage by creating the feelings you desire in people. Avoid unflattering expressions like rolling eyes, twitching your nose or knitting your eyebrows. These expressions aren't viewed favorably. Be mindful of the fact that your face is always sending signals.

One of the most important things to keep in mind if you want to come across as an effective, powerful and authoritative communicator is to always stay in control. Self-assured and assertive people are always in control of their emotions or know how to manage their emotions. They don't let their feelings or emotions get the better of them. Avoid the urge to keep checking on your phone or looking in the direction of the clock.

Turn your face and torso directly towards the person you are speaking to. Make consistent eye contact without coming across as intimidating or aggressive. Avoid actions that make you come across as nervous and edgy. For instance, chewing a pen, biting nails, tapping your feet and fidgeting nervously! It will take away from your credentials of being an effective and persuasive communicator.

Chapter 3:

How to Stay on the Same Foot While Communicating With People

We all know how painful it can feel to be misunderstood. You say something, but it gains an entirely different meaning for the other person, which leads to a series of unpleasantness, hostility, and conflict.

Like other errors and unpleasant situations, misunderstandings are nothing but errors that occur while perceiving. It is related to the multiple shortcuts developed by the human brain when it comes to making sense of our highly complex world. Remember, you get only one chance to make a sound first impression. If you blow it, too bad! Everyone likes to think they carefully take their time before making any judgments. If I asked you if you rush while forming an impression about someone, you would likely say no. However, the fact is, all of us make snap judgments about people. We are all guilty of making instant, knee-jerk impressions.

For instance, if you spot someone crying, rather than thinking that the person may have just heard some sad news or is having an awful day, we are prone to thinking that the person is naturally melancholic or down with depression. The reason first impressions are so inclined to quick judgments and misunderstandings is that our brains are naturally wired not to expend energy on things that don't matter or make a difference in our lives. If in the above example, the only information available to us is a person that is crying, making us believe the person to be a naturally weepy or depressed individual. Our brain does not want to spend energy thinking beyond that.

The real problem occurs when a person's behavior or actions doesn't tell us as much about them as our brain's knee-jerk reaction. Though incorrect first impressions can seldom be altered, there are plenty of workarounds for them.

To eliminate all this, here are some power tips to communicate effectively without leaving any scope for misunderstanding.

1. Know the Other Person's Triggers

There are particular words and phrases that can pave the way for plenty of misunderstanding. In your workplace, you may be referred to as "too nice", which may not be a positive label. It may simply imply you are someone who isn't strict with people, can't get work done from them or are not able to hold them accountable. This means each time someone refers to you as too nice you may view it in the same light as used by your co-workers. Maybe, someone else is known to be too nice in the same way professionally and when you refer to him or her as being too nice, they don't feel too flattered.

Know the other person's triggers so you don't get wrongly tripped over something harmless.

2. Rephrase

This holds good for avoiding being misunderstood as well as preventing any chances of misunderstanding the other person. When a person says something that isn't clear or you get the impression that what you are saying isn't apparent to the other person, merely rephrase what you just said. What I meant to say is so and so. Is it clear or do you need more clarity on the matter? Notice if they are acknowledging what you are saying through verbal and nonverbal gestures.

If you think the person is closed to the message you are trying to communicate (watch out for nonverbal cues like crossing arms and legs or fidgeting), stop the topic right there and start talking about something else to get them to open up. Once they appear more open, relaxed and receptive (again watch out for body language cues), get back to the tricky topic again. The idea is to draw them into a more receptive state of mind.

The person should be subconsciously more open to the idea of listening to you and believing you. Until you draw them back into this stance, don't go back to the original topic.

3. Identify the Level of Understanding of a Person

Whether you are addressing a large audience or talking to one person, try and establish their baseline level of understanding before going on a jargon-filled and technical rampage. These can create plenty of misunderstandings if the person isn't aware of these jargons or technical terms.

At times, you may assume the person knows specific terms and phrases and use them liberally throughout the conversation, only to discover they've assigned an entirely different meaning to what you've said. The decoder needs to understand what you've said in the right context. Try and have a general conversation or engage in small talk to understand the person's level of understanding.

4. Avoid Making Your Sentences Long Winded

Simplify what you want to say by keeping your sentences short and compelling. The more long-winded and verbose you make them; the lesser their impact will be. Plus by making it more complicated, you will increase your chances of being misunderstood. When the words, phrases, and sentences are kept simple, the probability of comprehending the message correctly is much more. Don't pump up or prep up sentences unnecessarily. They may lose their meaning.

5. Ask a Trusted Aide to be Brutally Honest

You want to know how others perceive you or how you appear to others, seek the help of a trusted friend. Urge them to be brutally honest when it comes to giving you feedback about the type of impression you make. This person should be trustworthy and someone who can offer genuine feedback. A person who knows you well will gain a good sense of where others may judge you correctly and where they may judge you incorrectly. This may be worth the trouble to see how the world at large perceives you. Let the friend have a mock conversation with you and point out specific instances where you are likely to be understood clearly and places where you are more likely to be misunderstood.

It isn't possible to immediately correct someone's first impression once they occur. However, you can over a period of time help people to see who you are. One of the best approaches to eliminate misunderstandings, when it happens at the beginning stages of an encounter, is to bombard the individual with evidence that they are incorrect. Yes, let them know all instances that are contrary to what they believe to be the truth about you.

It may take a while since people are prone to believe that you may be trying to manipulate their opinion of you. However, if you keep providing counter-evidence consistently, the person's brain can be rewired into changing their opinion. If you present someone with mounting evidence that runs past their initial impression of you, you'll create plenty of counter-information. The comfort of the new information will begin to build, and the person will be forced to evaluate their earlier assessment of you.

6. Get to the Point Quickly

Let's get this right, you aren't Beyoncé! So stop dancing wildly around a point or issue. Rambling, pausing too much, stammering, getting verbose and more is frustrating for the other person, and increases the potential of being misunderstood. If you want to say something meaningful, say it without rambling around in circles. If you are unable to get yourself to say something, stop right there and look for a better time to communicate when you are in a better position to say what you want.

Don't express yourself with a bunch of extras when you can keep it concise, sharp and effective. Beating about the bush will take away from the effectiveness of what you are trying to convey. Don't keep people guessing when you are talking about something important. Without appearing patronizing or condescending, ask them if they have understood what you are trying to say. Does this make sense to you? Do you understand what it is I am trying to convey? These are some questions you can ask to check the other person's level of understanding. Be patient and wait for a response from them. Try to make your way through the issue.

I know many people who suffer from verbal diarrhea. They say plenty of things without meaning it. This is paving the way for plenty of heartbreaks. When you say things without meaning it, you are setting the stage for being misunderstood and mistrusted every step of the way. Be honest and stick to your word. Being misunderstood also has a lot to do with context. It is influenced by everything from who the other person is, the nature of your equation with him or her and the type of emotions that are involved between the two. However, as a general rule never say what you don't mean.

7. Be a Great Listener

A good speaker is someone who is also an excellent listener. Effective communication is as much about developing your listening skills as your speaking skills.

Don't interrupt when a person is speaking. Interrupting a person can send a wrong message. It tells the other person that you are more important than them or that what they are saying is not as exciting as what you are saying. It can also convey you don't care about what the other thinks or feels, or that you don't have time to hear their opinion/take on a matter.

Isn't it amazing how some people turn a regular conversation into a contest that must be won? It isn't always about saying the best lines or having the last word. Some people don't believe in cooperating or collaborating but view everything as a competition. Instead of listening to other people, they will be thinking about what to say or framing their sentences when the other person is talking. They look to reply not to understand.

If you don't understand a thing, ask the speaker to go over it again. However, don't interrupt immediately. Wait for the speaker to pause. Once the speaker pauses, you can say something such as, "Wait a second, please. I didn't get what you just said about..." Offer acknowledgments to show you are keenly listening to the person. It can be anything from verbal nods to "hm" and "ah." The idea is to offer the speaker some clue that you are not just listening to him or her but also absorbing what they are saying.

One of the best acknowledgment tips is to reflect on the speaker's emotions or feelings by paraphrasing or validating what they said. "It must have been a terrible situation for you" or "You must be so happy!" or "I understand you are disturbed" are typical examples of acknowledging the speaker's feelings. Paraphrasing also works well. So what you are trying to say is......." This tells the speaker that you have been listening to them all along.

Keep an open mind and listen to the other person without succumbing to the temptation of judging and criticizing them. Sometimes, we feel an irresistible urge to throw in our two cents or give our opinion/suggestion about something as a person is peaking. At times what they say is even alarming! However, get out of the habit of mentally rating or judging what they are saying and just listen to them. Sometimes, all people want when they are speaking is a listening ear. They've probably already figured out what they want to do.

Unless the person is actively seeking your opinion or suggestions, avoid sharing it. Listen without making conclusions. Language is only a representation of the person's feelings and thoughts. You really don't know what is happening in a person's mind. Listen to them carefully to figure it out. Again, avoid being a sentence grabber. This is especially true when you are communicating with a person you know intimately. The urge to finish what they started saying is high. The speaker is led by his own train of thoughts, and you really don't know where it is headed. The person wants you to hear them not speak for them or throw in your two cents.

Empathy is crucial when it comes to being a good listener. Try and feel the emotions of a person while they are speaking, and express the same through facial expressions. For example, if the person is expressing sadness, your facial expressions should convey to him or her that you feel their sadness. This makes you come across as a concerned, empathetic and effective speaker.

Empathy is the cornerstone of active listening. Place yourself in the other person's shoes and feel the emotions and feelings the other person is undergoing at that moment. It paves the way for better communication. When the speaker realizes you are keenly listening to them and feeling their emotions, they are likelier to share more.

As a listener, you must be attentive yet relaxed. You don't have to keep staring at the person while he or she is talking. Look away occasionally, and then get back to the speaker. Stay attentive though. Nothing irks a speaker more than an inattentive listener! Be mentally present and give full attention to what the speaker is saying. Screen out disturbances like electronic gadgets and background noises. Again, the biggest distractions unknowingly come from within us. We are likelier to be distracted by our own thoughts, biases, and feelings.

Ask questions only to get a better understanding of what the person is trying to say and do not interrupt the flow of what the speaker is trying to communicate. Let's take an example. Say a co-worker Jill is telling you about a recent all girls trip she took to Europe. She's talking animatedly and excitedly about all the things she enjoyed there. In the course of her conversation, she mentions the name of a common friend Rose who was also with her on the trip. You jump in faster than you can say "Jill" and ask about Rose. "Oh, I haven't heard anything about her for a while, though last I heard was she was divorcing her abusive husband." Then the conversation shifts towards poor Rose, her unfortunate custody battle, the well-being of her children, domestic violence and family laws and more. Now, everything regarding Europe and Jill's holiday fades into oblivion.

Typically, this happens all the time. A person starts on one note, and the listener in his or zest for asking questions veers the topic in an entirely different direction. If as a speaker you notice that you've taken the subject elsewhere, take responsibility of bringing the conversation to the original topic by saying something along the lines of "It was nice to hear about Rose, tell me more about your fun adventures in Europe though."

Chapter 4:

Using Speech, Tone, and Pitch to Your Advantage

Your message is important but the manner in which you deliver it is probably even more critical if you want to be an effective communicator. The way you use intonation, pitch, tone, inflection and other elements adds more meaning to your message. In turn, giving it more character and making it more interesting.

1. Emphasize on the Right Word

This may sound unbelievable, but merely emphasizing the wrong word can send an entirely different message to the other person. Let us take a sentence like, "Did you steal my footwear?" Now the meaning of the phrase will keep changing depending on which word you emphasize on. Say, for instance, a person emphasizes on 'you' while asking this question, it implies the person is unsure about or wants to know whether you did it or someone else did it.

Similarly, if he or she emphasizes on 'steal' it may imply the person wants to know if you stole the book or simply borrowed it. Again, emphasizing on 'my' implies whether it was the person's or someone else's footwear that was stolen. Then focusing or emphasizing on 'footwear' may imply whether you stole the person's footwear or something else. Do you get the drift? Emphasizing the right word can make all the difference when it comes to conveying the correct meaning without falling prey to any misunderstandings.

2. Use Inflection to Your Advantage

Use intonation to communicate the right emotions about how you are feeling or the emotions you are experiencing. That doesn't mean you should speak in a sing-song manner all the time. It just means you should vary your tone/pitch high and low if you don't want to sound dull, or wish to communicate the right meaning of what you're trying to express. Intonation helps complement your words to know exactly how you are feeling.

It can also be used to convey that you are sure of what you are saying. It communicates to the other person whether you are commanding, requesting, suggesting or angry while speaking, which eliminates any potential misunderstandings. Imagine how unfortunate it will be if a harmless or straightforward request comes across as a command. Or if a mere suggestion makes it seem like you are ordering the person to do something or coming across as patronizing. This is precisely how misunderstandings in communication occur; when your intonation doesn't effectively communicate what you are trying to say.

Other than conveying the right meaning, intonation also makes your talk comes across as more interesting. It adds more color and character to your speech.

Again, there are three pitches while speaking. The high, middle or regular, and low! And there's nothing like the perfect pitch while talking. Play around with different pitches while speaking. Use them to your advantage for putting across your point compellingly and effectively.

3. Rate of Speech

One of the golden rules if you want to convey your point more effectively and compellingly is to maintain a steady and medium paced rate of speech (depending on your listener of course). If you speak too fast, people may not comprehend what you are saying. However, sputtering may make you come across as energetic, enthusiastic and alive. Listeners will try to grab a few words here and there but beyond that comprehension may seem tough.

Again, speaking slowly will make you sound serious, grim and emphatic. Listeners may catch every word, but they are sure to be bored to death waiting for you to finish. A slow speech can be used when you are trying to communicate an important point or when you want the other person to reflect upon what you've spoken. This can be used in combination with pausing at the right moment to give the listener more time to absorb your message.

4. Use Proper Pronunciation and Articulation

It is easy to understand correctly pronounced and articulated words. Faulty pronunciation is not just annoying; it also has the scope to lead to plenty of misunderstandings. Get familiar with using phonetics to articulate words in the right manner. You'll produce the correct sound and representation. Always open your mouth and speak. You'll be loud and audible. Move your mouth, jaw, and tongue freely. Aspirate sounds are meant to be aspirated for greater clarity. A single letter can have more than one sound. Also, be mindful of short and long sounds.

For instance, beet and bit are pronounced in different ways by pulling and constricting the sound. Similarly, "fool" and "full" are pronounced differently. The way in which words are pronounced change its meaning. Different pronunciations can give words different meanings.

The "th" is pronounced as soft "th" in "thin" and a harder "th" in "they". Similarly, "tin" and "thin" are not pronounced in the same way. Also, "day" is not the same as "they". Know the difference between pronouncing hard and soft consonants. One of the best ways to get this right is by practicing tongue twisters and doing mouth exercise. Remember this, articulate the right sounds without exaggerating it to avoid sounding fake.

5. Practice and Use 'PAIR'

Don't just remember these rules or study them, but actually implement them as discussed in the introduction. The idea is to put 'PAIR' into action. 'PAIR' is Pronunciation, Articulation, Inflection, and Rate. Start with the right articulation and volume.

Bring greater clarity to your speech, combine inflection and rate of speech to build a melody as one speaks. Practice on enhancing your 'PAIR' to come across as smart, confident and effective in your speech. Some of the most charismatic speakers use 'PAIR' to their advantage.

I share this tip with a lot of people. Record yourself while speaking to assess how you sound to others. Pay attention to your inflection, pronunciation, vocabulary, volume, and rate of speech. Another power-packed method is to practice in front of the mirror. Pay attention to your body language, mouth movements, gestures and expressions while talking. It will give you a good idea of the nonverbal signals you convey while communicating with others. Practice recording and speaking in front of the mirror to turn into an exceptional speaker or communicator.

6. Build a Powerful Vocabulary

One of the most essential elements of being a powerful communicator is to enrich your vocabulary. You should possess an extensive vocabulary to convert concepts or ideas into words or articulate your thoughts in a compelling manner. You can communicate what you want to express effortlessly if you have a rich vocabulary. A speaker also comes across as more exciting and confident when he or she uses different words. Think of it as the difference between a black and white photograph and a vivid, colorful image.

Having an incredible vocabulary allows the listener to paint a colorful picture in their mind about what the speaker is saying. It also helps avoid redundant words and phrases. However, one of the traps to guard against while enhancing your vocabulary is using complicated or highfalutin words just to sound impressive. The idea is to articulate your thoughts and feelings using the most compelling and appropriate words. This makes the right impact. If you use unnecessarily complex words, people may not understand what you are trying to communicate.

Challenge yourself to learn a new word each day. Keep a notebook to list down words, which can be highly effective. Remember the word by understanding its definition, stating it aloud and writing it in a book. You can also use a ton of vocabulary applications available on your smartphone.

Chapter 5:

Effective Communication in Personal Relationships

You've read this in every advice column, and it isn't really a secret—communication is the key of any successful, rewarding and gratifying relationship. I know it sounds similar to "just be yourself." But how does one really do that? It sounds amazing in theory and social media posters. However, how can it be applied in our practical, everyday life? Here are some practical and highly actionable tips and insights to increase your communication skills when it comes to personal relationships.

1. Avoid Communicating When Under High Stress

In high-stress situations, we often say or do things we later regret. Happens all the time, right? There is also a tendency to take everything that a person says personally. Our judgment becomes skewed, and we lose our sense of logic. Instead, focus on returning to a calm state of mind before addressing the issue or concern. You'll think more and speak more coherently.

You won't end up saying things you'll regret or that will further aggravate the problem. When you are in a calm and relaxed state of mind, you'll know whether to respond to the situation or remain silent. Use stalling techniques. Offer yourself some time to think and go over the issue. Pause for a while and collect your thoughts. Pausing is better than rushing into a response only to say the wrong things. The golden rule of communication within personal relationships is to avoid saying anything under stress and duress. Wait to calm down and then make your points in a coherent and logical manner.

Of course, it is easier said than done because strong emotions are involved. However, each time you find yourself getting stressed or angry, just keep a technique ready to gain more calmness. For example, when things get heated up and stressed, some people just like going out and walking for a few minutes before getting back to the discussion. They come back calmer and less stressed.

Even in the middle of a heated argument or discussion, don't lose your balance. Speak coherently, keep an even tone and make eye contact with the person you are addressing. Your body language should be relaxed, unperturbed and open. Don't reveal any signs of nervousness, anxiety or stress through your body language. When you notice that things are getting emotionally intense, swing into action to bring down the level of emotional intensity! Bring down stress, manage your feelings and act appropriately.

Our body automatically gives out signals when we feel stressed and anxious. Your muscles will feel tighter. The hands will slowly clench. Your breathing becomes shallower. These are all physical symptoms of stress. Take a deep breath and calm down. If you are not up for it, postpone the conversation or take a short break before getting back to it.

Sensory experiences are one of the best ways to kill momentary stress. Through sensory experiences including sound, smell, sight, taste, and movement, you can beat stress. For instance, pop a candy in your mouth and notice how it tastes. How about taking a few deep breaths? Or visualizing a happy memory! These are sensory-rich experiences that can help reduce your stress. Every person has a different response to sensory inputs. Identify things that relax and soothe you.

2. Be Assertive

Being assertive doesn't mean you fight with your loved ones on every issue that comes up. It simply means standing up for yourself and not let people walk all over you. Being assertive in personal relationships helps you set boundaries and prevents people from taking you for granted. It also paves the way for clear communication, decision-making and increasing your self-esteem.

Assertive people express their thoughts in an honest,

confident and open manner. They stand up for themselves and respect others around them. Being assertive should not be mistaken for being hostile, demanding, dogmatic or aggressive. It is about understanding the other person and being understood without focusing on winning the argument. An assertive communicator will always attempt to come up with a middle way rather than being obsessed with winning an argument or forcing their opinion on the other person.

How does one develop greater assertiveness to communicate effectively in personal relationships? Value yourself and your views/opinion. Understand that they are as important as the other person's. Identify your needs and wants and learn to express them without trampling on other people's rights. Learn to express even negative thoughts in a positive way. Stay respectful even when you are involved in an ugly feud with a person. This gets people to listen to you and take your words seriously. Being disrespectful takes away from your credibility, while also making people switch off after a while!

One of the most important things for being an assertive communicator is to know your limits and to say no when you mean no. Don't let people take advantage of you. When you aren't up for something, politely, firmly and respectfully say no. Look for solutions where everyone will feel happy with the outcome.

Demonstrate an empathetic assertion in personal

relationships, where you acknowledge the other person's feelings but also express yours freely and clearly. For example, "I understand that you've been working very hard, but I also want you to make .... for us." Then there's escalating assertion, which can be used when your initial attempts to be assertive are not successfully met. For instance, "If you don't stick to what we've mutually agreed about your addiction and abusive ways, I will be forced to consider separation/divorce." This is different from threatening a person. You are merely stating the consequences if your rights or needs are overlooked.

I know some people aren't naturally assertive or don't have a confident personality. It can be developed with practice. Start by practicing in lower risk scenarios to build up the confidence and skills for high-risk situations. Practice assertiveness techniques on people whom you trust and who are capable of giving you honest feedback.

3. Focus on Collaborative Communication

One of the most significant problems of communication in personal relationships during modern times is a misconception where the objective of communication is concerned. Most view it as a battle or debate between two parties, when in fact, the idea is to cooperate and collaborate and not compete.

The purpose of communication is, therefore, determining what the real situation is. Communication involves collaborating as both the parties share their feelings, perception, ideas, and thoughts to arrive at a correct understanding of what happened.

While approaching a conversation with your partner, disarm. This simply means give up your obsession to be right or win the argument. This isn't a war that has to be won. I any damage is done you both lose. Again, on the other side, this doesn't mean you have to compromise or give in to everything he or she says. You obviously have the right to feel the emotions you feel. However, all the same, think that your partner may have something to say worth hearing or considering. Stop treating every conversation as a battleground where you have to prove you are right all the time. There is no real victory in these situations.

4. Identify the Other Person's Communication Style and Your Own

Recognizing your and the other person's communication style is one of the best ways to communicate more effectively with them while also eliminating instances of misunderstanding and conflict. Here are some primary communication styles that can be identified and built upon to accomplish more harmonious and fulfilling interactions.

Assertive communicators. These are people who possess a high sense of self-esteem, self-assuredness, and self-confidence.

This is known to be the healthiest communication style that seeks to work out a middle way between being too passive or aggressive while also staying away from manipulation games.

Assertive people realize their limits and don't want to be pushed around by people who want to use them to get things done. All the same, they won't violate other people's emotions or rights to fulfill their purpose. The assertive communicator style is win-win because confident communicators come up with solutions that are beneficial for everyone involved, compared to merely thinking about their own needs.

Typical characteristics of an assertive communicator—they accomplish goals without hurting others; they protect their own rights while also being respectful of other people's rights. They are more socially and emotionally expressive. Assertive communicators make their own choices and accept responsibility for these choices.

Their typical nonverbal behavior includes medium pitch, volume, and speed of speech. Their posture is open, relaxed, and symmetrical. They stand tall, and there are barely any signs of fidgeting or nervousness. Their gestures are open, expansive and rounded. Assertive people typically make good eye contact and maintain a spatial position that conveys they are respectful of others and in control.

Typical things they say include, "Please would you lower the volume? I am finding it tough to focus on my work" or "I am sorry I won't be able to help with your homework because I have an appointment scheduled with my physician." Try and be an assertive communicator if you want to be effective.

Aggressive communicators. This style is all about winning— unfortunately at other people's expense. Aggressive communicators act like their needs are supreme, and nothing or no one else matters. They behave like they are born with greater rights, and have a bigger say in things than others around them. Predictably, this isn't an effective communication style. Since aggressive communicators focus excessively on the delivery of their message, the content is invariably lost.

Their nonverbal behavior includes loud volume, bigger and more expansive posture than other people, fast and jerky facial expressions and a spatial position that invades other people's space or tries to stand upon other people. Typical language used by them includes "you are insane" or "this has to be done in my way" or "you make me mad." Blaming, taunting, name-calling, insulating, sarcasm and threatening are all characteristics of an aggressive communicator.

Passive-aggressive communicators. These communicators appear passive on the outside but are actually playing out their anger 'behind the scenes.' These people generally feel powerless and are mostly resentful. They subtly undermine targets of their resentment, often even at the cost of sabotaging themselves.

Passive aggressive will typically say things like "why don't you move ahead and do this. My ideas aren't of any value anyway" or "you always know more than others anyway." There is a hint of sarcasm in what they say.

Their body language involves speaking in a sugar sweet voice, maintaining an asymmetrical posture, jerky and quick gestures and facial expressions that appear sweet and innocent. The passive aggressive spatial position involves standing too close. At times, even touching other people while pretending to be friendly, warm and affable!

Submissive communicators. Submissive communicators are about pleasing people and avoiding confrontation at any cost. They will bend backward to please other people often at the cost of their own wants and needs. Typically, submissive communicators place other people's needs before theirs. They believe their needs aren't as crucial as people around them. This leads to disillusionment and frustration. Typical language used by them includes, "Oh! It's really nothing, don't worry" or "Oh! Its fine, I really don't want it any longer" or "You pick, anything is alright with me."

Typical submissive communicator body language includes a soft volume, diminutive, head down posture, fidgeting gestures, and a spatial position that makes them appear lower in stature than others. It is marked by an evident victim mentality, and refusal to try initiatives for improving things.

Manipulative communicator. Manipulative communicators are shrewd, scheming and calculating. They prey upon other people's feelings and emotions to serve their purpose. Manipulative communicators possess the ability to influence and control people for their own benefit. The words they speak almost always have underlying or hidden messages, which their victims are unaware of.

Their typical verbiage includes, "you are so fortunate to enjoy these delicious chocolates. I wish I were lucky enough to have them too. I can't afford such pricey chocolates" or "I didn't have time to purchase anything, so I had no option but to wear this attire. I am crossing my fingers that I don't look too bad in it." Their voice is patronizing, often bordering on envious, high-pitched and ingratiating, while facial expressions are typically "hangdog."

5. Use "I" Statements

Of course, you want to express your feelings, desires, and needs. It is an important part of being an assertive communicator. You can express your needs, desires, and feelings without attributing blame to the other person. This is one of the biggest secrets of communicating effectively in personal relationships. You can communicate what you want to say without offending the other person by using "I" statements instead of "You" statements.

By using "I" instead of "You", you take responsibility for your actions rather than passing on the blame to another person. It is direct, non-accusatory and honest. It emphasizes the person's behavior and it's after effects. "I" statements comprise talk about the other person's behavior, your feelings, and consequences. Typically, it is like "I feel……. when…….because……… " Or "even I feel…….when you……….and would prefer……….."

Be specific when you are referring to another person's behavior, refer to a current or recent incident instead of generalizing it. Ensure you own your feelings, and that you accept responsibility for your feelings rather than accusing others. No one can make you feel something. Keep your body language and tone calm, relaxed and open. Avoid making these statements in a more passive-aggressive or sarcastic manner. It won't come across as genuine.

Some example of accusatory "you" statements and "I" statements are as follows. While blaming "you statements" state something like, "you are working late again, just like always." The same statement can be converted into an "I" statement by saying something like, "I feel frustrated when you work late because it doesn't allow me to spend more time with you." Similarly, instead of saying "you don't love me anymore", try saying something like, "I feel lonely when you stop calling me for long periods. Can we work something out so I don't feel like this anymore?"

See what we are doing here? We are accepting responsibility for our feelings instead of blaming or accusing the other person. You are telling the other person that you are experiencing a particular feeling rather than them being responsible for it. You are expressing your desire without pointing the finger at the other person, which works wonders.

6. Make Small Talk

Yes I know it's your partner of 20 years, a family member or a close person we are talking about here and not a stranger you've just met at a party. However, if experts are to go by, small talk about seemingly insignificant details have a more substantial impact on your emotional ties than so-called, profound or deep emotional conversations. Psychoanalyst Harry Stack Sullivan created an approach that he referred to as "detailed inquiry", where he recommended therapists to accumulate as much information about a client's life as possible to find clues about his or her personality.

Research conducted by John Gottman and Janice Driver researched this suggestion with a group of married folks and discovered that boring or mundane details or the seemingly trivial moments which are a part of a couple's everyday life have a greater bearing on a relationship's health than emotionally serious and so-called meaningful conversations. This makes making small talk with your partner an excellent idea!

Similarly, research published in Psychological Science reveals that we connect better with others when we are able to talk about everyday experiences. Say, for instance, you are attempting to repair a ruptured relationship or marriage, start with the children. Speak about positive memories and amusing/cute incidents related to your children. Avoid referring to moments of conflict or discord. Find shared memories and moments—this can be one of the most effective solutions when it is about a child you both adore.

7. Listen, Listen, Listen

This is all the more critical when it comes to our personal relationships. Since we are so used to having the person around us, many times, we just take what they are saying for granted and don't practice active listening. Knowing that what you are saying is being keenly heard is one of the best feelings in the world. It brings about a sense of connection between people.

One way to sharpen your listening skills is to practice active listening. You are not just nodding your head and offering verbal acknowledgments, but you also comprehend what is being said. Understanding can be conveyed through everything from your smile to a word or a phrase, to whatever unique nonverbal cues you use to communicate you are listening to the other person. Active listening also comprises interrupting the other person while he or she is speaking or asking for clarifications (which reveal you have been listening to the other person).

Disagreements also signify active listening. But how can you disagree with a person if you haven't heard what he or she is speaking about? If you are interrupting the person to seek permission, say something like, "sorry for interrupting you but can I ask you something?" This is a reasonable request if you want to ask something when the person hasn't finished speaking yet. If you're going to disagree with the person, wait until they've made all their points or finished speaking.

They may have something that you may agree with at the end of their talk, so hold on until the end to disagree. If you feel that they haven't described something accurately, seek more clarification rather than downright accusing them of manipulation, lies or deceit. You may gain greater clarity by asking them more questions.

Conclusion

Thank you for reading or listening to this book.

I sincerely hope it has offered you multiple techniques and strategies about communicating effectively across settings to enjoy more lasting, harmonious and fulfilling relationships.

The objective of the book is to help you get rid of your inhibitions, nervousness, and insufficient confidence to take on the world more confidently and effectively, one communication skill at a time. Communication is the key towards building solid, rewarding and lasting relationships along with determining your chances of success in life.

The next step is to start using the strategies mentioned in this book right away—which we spoke about in the introduction. Information must be translated into knowledge, which in turn is converted into experience and wisdom. Of course, you won't transform from an awkward communicator into a confident communicator overnight. However, one step a time you'll get closer to your goal. With application and practice, you'll slowly, but inevitably, transform into a communication force to be reckoned with!

Conversation Skills

Useful Methods and Advice to Conquer Small Talk, Improve Social Confidence and Network Like Never Before

Keith Coleman

Introduction

Conversation skills are something that many people struggle with. And the thing is, you *need* to master this skill in order to thrive in your everyday life and workplace where you spend the majority of your time. You might say that conversation skills are an essential skill every individual should improve upon. But how do we do that if making smooth and effortless discussions is something we struggle with?

The answer is through repetitive practice of effective strategies. Master these methods to start noticing a massive difference in the way you communicate with those around you. Be it verbal or non-verbal, effective communication is one asset that everybody should have in their repertoire, and in this book you will discover the essential techniques, strategies and methods to help you improve, even the non-verbal messages that you might not be aware of (yes, they matters just as much).

If you're tired of struggling to keep a conversation going, initiate a discussion or to fit in at social gatherings, then this book might have precisely what you need. Even if you're an introvert by nature, you will benefit from what this book has to teach. Start building genuine relationships and network like never before with useful methods and advice to conquer small talk while improving your self-confidence in the process.

Chapter 1:

Why Effective Communication Skills Matter

Having a conversation and being an effective communicator matter. You know that, which is why you are here right now reading this book. Picture this scenario:

You're in the middle of a conversation with someone. Unfortunately, that person is not the best at having a discussion. They're stumbling and struggling to get the point across, their words become jumbled, and they're becoming increasingly more nervous until finally, the conversation tapers off into awkward silence. An awkward silence then leads to forced attempts at filling in the gaps with mindless chit-chat to which neither party is interested in. Finally, both people go their separate ways, relieved to have left that uncomfortable situation.

What do you think is going to happen? You can try to be as courteous as possible, but eventually, you're going to struggle to maintain interest in the conversation. This is a common issue, particularly for those who have not the best skills with social interactions.

But don't be too hard on yourself. Not everyone is a natural at charming people, especially strangers that they meet for the first time. Introverts might even have a harder time with that sort of thing. Having absolutely nothing in common to talk about can be straight up terrifying.

Let's Talk About *Why* Conversation Skills Matter in Everyday Scenarios

We encounter dozens of people each day when we leave our homes. We pass them on the street, in the supermarkets, department stores or when making a purchase. And we encounter people day-in and day-out at the workplace where — if you have a full-time job - demands you be in the office for at least 8 hours a day. Naturally, you'll have to converse with someone at some point, which is precisely why having some skills matter.

We live in a world in which we are surrounded by people, and you *need* to be able to relate to others around you. Whether you enjoy it or not, you *need* to be able to converse with people to help you get what you want and where you want to go.

Conversation skills help you to form bonds and relationships with the people around you, to make you feel connected and give you a sense of belonging. Communication is one of the essential foundations of a human relationship and determines just how well you can bond with another person. It helps two strangers become friends. It keeps you from feeling isolated like you're completely lost and alone with no one around who understands you.

Have you ever found yourself in a situation where you've had a misunderstanding with someone because the information was taken out of context? These types of circumstances can escalate into arguments and in the most severe cases even lead to physical confrontation. This is one example of why it's so important to be able to converse well to get your point across, to be clearly understood by whomever you may speak to.

Why Conversation Skills Matter at Work

Think of all the successful individuals you know, whether directly or indirectly, for example motivational speakers. What contributes to their success? How did they get to where they are? Because they are able to communicate effectively, and they have mastered the art of conversation skills to a point where they can meet anybody in a completely relaxed, effortless manner. They are easily understood and easy to get along with. They command attention when they speak and more importantly, they project an air of confidence with every conversation. That is what great conversation skills can do for you.

Being able to converse well also helps you to express your ideas, especially at a workplace where it could actually give your career a boost. In a work environment, your performance is reliant on how well you can contribute productively to your team and your organization, to be seen as an asset.

Conversation skills at the workplace are just as valuable as any other skill set you're already utilizing to keep you in your job. No matter how good you may be at what you do, you're not going to get very far if you're unable to communicate well with the people you work with.

One example of this would be a scenario where you would have to deal with an unhappy or dissatisfied client. Imagine not being able to communicate well in that situation where you would have to persuade or try to appease them. Struggling to convey your message correctly might make the client even more unhappy or angry with your service, leading them to take their business elsewhere. In a work environment, poor conversation skills spell disaster and can possibly even end your career.

Are you starting to understand why conversation skills are so critical? Do you see just how essential they can be?

Working on these skills and being able to small talk will help you develop the confidence you need to form relationships for networking. Keeping your relation with your co-workers harmonious and productive helps you to feel comfortable and confident working and sharing ideas with them. This also goes the other way around, small talk helps your colleagues being at ease and comfortable in your presence. They will never be worried about awkward pauses and feeling discomfort when you don't know what to say to each other. At work, you'll become the person that is approachable and likable. And when a conversation is at a point where it can flow freely, it becomes easier to build a working environment or a team that's cohesive and productive.

Conquering small talk will make you an asset to your organization, especially if you're dealing with clients. Building a strong rapport that results in sales, loyalty and returning customers rely heavily on effective communication. If you can master these skills, every client that deals with you will walk away feeling satisfied and happy with the service they received. Opening up a conversation that leads you to understand exactly what they want makes it much easier to fulfill their requests.

How Do I Even Start With Small Talk If I'm Terrible at It?

That is precisely what you will come to learn by the time you get through this book. The first key point to remember when learning how to conquer small talk and conversations is <u>timing</u>. You need to start a discussion off on the right foot with someone from the very beginning.

Before you strike up a conversation with someone, you need to observe and gauge the situation. Pay attention to every detail. For instance, is the person you intend to have a conversation with busy? Are they distracted? Are they preoccupied with something else? Are they already in the middle of a conversation? Is this the right time or situation to attempt talking to them?

Taking the situations mentioned above into consideration, the following advice will help you to get established as a memorable and likable person, someone that they would enjoy talking to again:

1. Remembers Their Names

The best way to be impressionable right from the get-go is to be someone who remembers another person's name. When you begin a small talk session, walk up to that person, smile, and make eye contact when you're introducing yourself. Make it a habit of remembering their names. That way, the next time you hold a conversation with them, and you show that you can remember who they are, they'll warm up to you immediately, kicking off that session on the right foot.

One useful trick to remembering someone's name is to repeat it back to them when they introduce themselves. For example, after they have told you their name, say *I'm pleased to meet you, Anne.* End the conversation the same way, by repeating their name once more, *it was lovely talking to you, Anne, I hope we can do it again.* Think about how you've felt when someone remembered your name as opposed to when you've had to re-introduce yourself to someone you've already met. Which one is going to leave more of an impression? You need to *make* people *want* to talk to you again.

2. Be Present in The Conversation

This may not be a big important business meeting that requires your full-on, 100% attention, but small talk is just as essential and commands just as much of your attention. In fact, make it a habit each time you're talking with someone to give them your undivided attention. Put away your phone, ignore everything else, and focus entirely on the person you are speaking to.

Conversation is a two-way street, and if you're not an active participant in it, then it won't be long before you eventually run out of things to say. The conversation will be filled with awkward silences and gaps before finally tapering off and die. You need to be able to bounce back and forth, keeping the conversation flowing, so the other person is not the only one doing all the talking. Pay attention and actively listen when the other person is speaking. Process the information they are giving you, which will help you to keep an active conversation going. This leaves the other person feeling good because they'll perceive that they matter and will be excited to talk to you again.

3. Be Genuine

The easiest way to do this is by being yourself. Even though you are practicing and putting the strategies you learn into effect, be wary of trying too hard or you might come off as insincere or fake. Think about a time when you thought a person speaking to you seemed to be like that. How did it make you feel? If you're attempting to offer a compliment of some sort make sure it is one that is sincere or don't bother saying anything at all, or you may risk coming off as dishonest. Why is it risky to offer a compliment you don't mean? Remember how we talked about non-verbal communication earlier? If you don't mean what you say, it's going to show in your body language. The bottom line is this, be genuine all the way.

Chapter 1 Summary

Conversation skills matter because:

- Being able to effectively communicate and converse with others around you help form bonds and relationships.

- Effective conversation skills minimize instances of misunderstanding and communication.

- Effective conversation skills help you to increase your confidence when talking to other people.

Conversation skills matter at work because:

- Conversation skills help you to better express your ideas and opinions.

- Conversation skills and small talk help building relationships and rapport with clients and colleagues alike.

- Effective conversation and communication lead to better teamwork when people are comfortable being around you.

- Effective conversation skills help you to maintain relationships and network with your clients.

Advice to remember when beginning your journey:

- The key to starting a conversation off on the right foot from the beginning is all about your timing. Wait for the right time, and make sure the person is in the right frame of mind to be approached and engaged in small talk.

- Be genuine; don't offer compliments unless you are entirely sincere about it.

- Actively participate and listen in the conversations you are involved in.

- Make an effort to remember the names of the people you are conversing with.

- Don't try too hard. Remember, what you are saying with your body language is more visible than you might think.

Chapter 2:

Communication Obstacles you're Likely to Face

Being able to hold a productive conversation seems to be enough of a struggle for many people, a struggle which is made even more complicated by certain obstacles. Misunderstanding and miscommunication will happen because of these difficulties we are faced with. No matter how hard we try, sometimes our messages get lost along the way and do not come across how we may have intended them to.

Common Communication Obstacles That Are Likely to Cause a Problem in Your Conversation Attempts

A lack of confidence, not carrying yourself assertively during a conversation is considered as one of the more prominent barriers, because the receiving party will not be convinced with what you have to say. Chapter 6 highlights and discusses this in more detail. Besides lacking confidence, some other obstacles which are considered a hindrance:

1. Not Paying Attention

Have you ever found it hard to concentrate halfway through a conversation? Those moments where you find yourself momentarily blanking out or thinking about something else, and when you snap back to the discussion you see that you've missed half the story. It often happens; sometimes our minds just tend to wander off, especially if a conversation isn't riveting enough to hold our attention. That's when the problem occurs because drifting in and out during a conversation means you're potentially missing crucial parts of information.

2. Different Accents and Jargons

The world is a diverse melting pot these days, and we come across people from all sorts of different countries from around the world. Communicating with individuals who are so different from us can be an incredible learning experience, but it can also prove to be a considerable conversation barrier, especially when different accents are involved. Small talk can be confusing when you have trouble understanding a person because they pronounce certain words differently or use jargons which we may not understand. A small talk session is not going to be useful if you or the other party always have to apologize and ask for the question or statement to be repeated.

3. Getting Distracted During

Having your phone ring in the middle of a conversation is another example of a communication barrier. Or if you're in the middle of a crowded area with lots of noise going on, people talking and phones continually beeping is also not an ideal situation. Straining to be heard will hardly lead to a great session. If you're talking to someone, there's nothing more off-putting than to see them being distracted by their devices or what is going on around them instead of being focused on you.

4. Talking in A Rushed or Hasty Manner

Have you ever had someone just rushing through a message and you knew they were just trying to get it over and done with because they had something else to do? That is a communication obstacle when a conversation is being hurried or rushed to an end. Not only is the person you are conversing with going to feel disturbed by your attitude, but by rushing through what you want to say, you place yourselves at risk of missing out on vital bits of information. Even if it's small talk, treat it in the same manner that you would with an important client meeting. If you can't give that conversation your full attention then don't start it at all.

5. Too Much Information

Bombarding your listener with too much information at once is another communication obstacle you want to be careful to avoid if you hope to become an active conversationalist. You should not overload your listener with too much information since not everyone can process the amount they receive in the same way. Some people may be able to absorb information quickly, while others need more time to make sense of what they are being presented with. If you go all out and bombard your listener, you're going to make them feel overwhelmed and disengaged from the conversation.

Okay, So What Can I Do to Be Better at Conversation Despite These Obstacles?

Glad you asked. Now that you're aware of some of the common obstacles, we can work on overcoming them and improving your conversation skills. The following strategies will help you accomplish this:

1. Think About the Listener

While you may think you are easy enough to understand, remember that not everyone responds to information and conversation in the same way. Have you ever noticed that you don't necessarily talk to two people in the same manner? Some jokes, for example, you would share with specific friends because you know they would get it, but you wouldn't necessarily share that same joke with another group of friends. That's an example of how some conversational messages need to be tweaked according to the audience, and this is a skill that you need to learn. Part of being a great conversationalist is knowing your audience and how to adjust what you're saying to be understood and well received.

2. Be Clear About What You're Trying to Say

It helps your conversation if you are clear about what you want to say before you attempt to convey your message to someone else. For example, try writing it down instead of just holding your thoughts in your head. When you write down what you plan to say (and this method works if you have time to prepare, such as before a networking event for example). It gives you a chance to clearly see the message you want to say, and you'll be able to get a better judgment about whether your points come across clearly or not. It also gives you an excellent chance to see if you've missed out on any crucial points and it gives you time to practice what you want to say. If you don't have the time to prepare before a conversation or small talk session, then try to keep your sentences short and avoid using any complicated words or jargon.

3. Don't Contradict Yourself

Nothing is a conversation killer quite like someone who contradicts themselves when they're talking. Keeping your points and the topic of your conversation consistent is how you become great at small talk. If you start contradicting yourself during a discussion, your listener is going to be confused about exactly what you're trying to tell them. They will gradually lose interest and not be inclined to engage in a conversation with you after that since they won't see you as trustworthy. An example of this could be at the workplace when you're trying to communicate with a client, you need to be clear about your company's mission, vision and what it stands for and why they should sign up for the service you are providing. They cannot do that if your messages and style of communication are unclear and contradictory.

4. Using All the Right Words

It's not just about how you say it, but what you mean that is just as important, if not more so. Your choice of words during a conversation will determine just how well it goes. Again, this goes back to communicating effectively and getting your points across as clearly as you possibly can. One way you can do this is by keeping your words and sentences simple, direct and to the point. Don't beat around the bush and make circles and loops telling unrelated points, anecdotes or stories before you get to the main point.

5. Be Confident

But not to a point where you come off as having an air of superiority or be perceived as an overconfident person. You need to find the balance between having just enough confidence, while at the same time making yourself seem approachable so that people want to talk and be around you. Examples of being overconfident are when you come off looking like a show-off or a know-it-all, as it's often the case with someone who is well-versed and familiar with the subject of discussion. They might begin to *tell* instead of *share*. Instead of becoming a conversational information exchange, it becomes a conversation with one person saying the listener how things should be.

6. Keeping Your Body Language Open and Welcoming

When you're about to engage in small talk with someone, especially someone you're unfamiliar with, you need to remind and convince yourself that you are excited about having this conversation and you're eager and curious to see what you can learn from someone else. This is so that your mind and body will work as one, being open, welcoming and inviting. The next time you're out with friends, take note of what your body language is like. It's probably relaxed, comfortable and no arms are crossed because you're at ease and relaxed with the people you're talking to. This is the kind of body language you need to project with *every* conversation you engage in, not just the ones you have with friends. Keeping your body language open, warm and inviting will entice others to want to participate in a conversation with you, they'll subconsciously respond to the body language that you are emitting.

7. Be A Good Listener

Conquering small talk and become an excellent conversationalist is not just about what you say, but it's also about how well you *receive* information. Being an active listener is one of the critical tools a good conversationalist always has. They know that listening to what others have to say is all a part of the active communication process. If you're just doing all the talking without listening, you're not going to be much of a conversationalist right? Besides, if you can't listen effectively, you're going to end up missing out on the information you might need to develop a social interaction beyond small talk.

8. Start Making Small Talk a Habit

If you're only working on improving your skills in forced encounters, then it's going to take you a long time before you start to see any progress. A tip is to make small talk a habit by putting it into practice at every chance you get. Each encounter is an occasion to engage in a conversation with someone, an opportunity to hone your skills. Make mental notes about how you think you did, how the other person responded and what you think you can improve upon your next try.

9. Subtly Copy the Person You're Talking To

If you're feeling nervous during a small talk session then try the following: subtly but discreetly mimic the mannerisms of the person you are speaking too, especially if they happen to be a more confident person. This is sometimes known as mirroring, and what this does is let the person you're having a talk with know that you feel comfortable in their presence. This helps to create a relaxed situation even if you feel a bit nervous.

Chapter 2 Summary

Communication barriers and obstacles will happen from time to time, despite your best efforts. Here are the key points you need to remember to reduce those obstacles to a minimum:

- Think about the messages you convey. Are they clear enough to be understood by whoever is listening to you?

- Learn how to tweak your messages according to your audience, because not everyone understands or interprets signals in the same manner.

- When you're talking, think about your listener and how they might be receiving your messages. Put yourself in their shoes and think, *Am I able to understand myself?*

- Be clear about what you want to communicate to avoid contradicting yourself, or risk making the listener lose confidence in you and your message.

- Try to use the right/best words that will get your point across in the most precise way.

- Don't bombard and overload your listener with too much information all at once, because you might risk making them feel overwhelmed. Pace yourself. There's no need to get everything out there all at once.

- Don't rush through what you're trying to say or attempt to communicate hurriedly. If you don't have the time to spare, avoid engaging in a small talk conversation.

- Keep distractions to a minimum so you can pay attention to the person you are talking to.

- Avoid engaging in small talk in an environment that is noisy and filled with distractions. If it's not the right time or place, hold off until later.

- Be an active listener and give your full attention to whoever you may be speaking to.

- Put your phone on silent and minimize anything that can distract you when you're attempting to engage in a small talk conversation.

- Be confident, but not to a point where you come off seeming like a superior know-it-all.

- Keep your body language warm, open and inviting throughout every conversation you have, much like how you do when you're with a group of friends.

- Start making small talk a habit by actively engaging in practice sessions at every opportunity, even if the person you're talking to doesn't know that you're practicing. With each practice session, take note of how people responded to you, how well you think you did and what you think you can improve upon next time.

- If small talk sessions still make you nervous, a good strategy is to mimic the mannerisms of the person you're talking to, especially if they have more confidence.

Chapter 3:

Getting Started on Building Effective Conversation Skills

It would be great if we were all born with the gift of being a natural speaker. We may not possess the skills just yet, but the good news is that conversation and small talk is something that can be *developed*.

Everyone can learn how to conquer small talk with the right methods and strategies at their disposal, whether it's in everyday life or at work.

I'm Ready to Begin Conquering Small Talk, Let's Do This!

You already have to communicate and converse with people almost daily. Now is the time to fine-tune those skills to become even better, to a point where you can small talk with complete strangers and still have the conversation flowing smoothly as if you've known each other all along. Forget mindless chit-chat, these small talk sessions should be productive since you never know what networking opportunities they may lead to.

To start improving your conversational skills, here is what you need to do:

1. Be Adaptable and Flexible

In Chapter Two, we talked about how you wouldn't necessarily speak to one group of friends the way that you would with another. You talk to your friends, family, co-workers, and strangers differently; it's not just one style of speaking. Being adaptable and flexible, able to change your manner and form to suit the audience that you're dealing with is how you become a great conversationalist. The key here is to tailor each message to suit your audience. So, before you even commence your conversation session (especially with people you don't know that well), you need to make a quick assessment about who you're going to speak to and how you should approach them.

2. Keep it Concise

The best way to make yourself clearly understood to your audience during small talk sessions is to keep your sentences, words, and manner as clear and concise as possible. Nobody likes listening to long-winded stories, especially if they have just met you or you're in a work-networking type of situation. To conquer small talk, you need to become someone who people want to have a conversation with and enjoy talking to. This means you need to start practicing becoming someone that gets right to the point when needed. If a piece of information is unimportant, then you probably can skip it. Stick to the facts and the points, and you'll do just fine.

3. Block Out Distractions

When attempting to engage someone in a conversation, always make sure both parties are in the right frame of mind and environment. For example, if there's too much distraction going on, then it's probably best to not engage right there and then. Before engaging in a conversation with someone, ensure that you don't have any pressing matters that may demand your attention, these will likely cause you to exit the conversation sooner than you might want to.

4. Don't Be a Mumbler

Mumbling and stumbling are not considered a desirable skill for obvious reasons. To be an excellent conversationalist, you need to speak openly and definitively, even projecting your voice if needed. Practice by yourself in the mirror, pretending you're conversing with someone. Record yourself on your mobile phone to see how you sound. Are you able to clearly understand everything you're saying? Does it make any sense?

5. Changing the Way You Think

Before picking this book up, you've probably had some low self-esteem related to social interactions. Now it's time to change your mindset and reframe your thoughts about yourself. The first step is to believe you are a great speaker. Confidence is going to make a huge difference, and a person cannot be confident if they are consistently filled with doubt. The minute you start to question yourself, put a stop to it and say, *I CAN do this*. You need to repeatedly persuade yourself until you believe it. It's entirely up to you to build up your confidence, nobody will do it for you.

6. Visualizing Yourself Succeeding

Don't knock it until you've tried it. Visualization is a concept preached by many successful individuals *because it works*. Unfortunately, visualization is underestimated and not used enough. Think you can't visualize? Think again. If you can picture all the things that might go wrong in a situation, you can most certainly do the opposite by portraying yourself succeeding. Visualize yourself in a small talk session with someone. Imagine with clarity all the things you're saying, what you're talking about, and imagine it going great. Keep doing this exercise, training your mind to become better and better until it is no longer a struggle

7. Be Prepared

The most successful and confident individuals are the ones who are always prepared for every situation. If up until now you were just winging it with your small talk sessions then it's time to put a little work in beforehand. Preparing for a prior business meeting, client meeting or network session is easy because you'll already know what to expect and what type of people that will attend. Preparing for individuals you might meet without warning is a little trickier, but it can be done. How? By arming yourself with knowledge of topics which will make good conversation starters. Research and read about the latest general happenings, your surroundings and other issues which would do well as a conversation starter. Being prepared will help with situations where you find yourself stumbling at a loss for what to talk about. You'll gradually gain confidence with each successful encounter.

8. Be Present

Do this wholly and wholeheartedly when you're talking to another person. Being there doesn't just mean being there physically and going through the motions, it means being there mentally if you want to truly engage in a meaningful conversation with someone. The other party can tell whether you're giving them your full attention, or if your mind is distracted and thinking about something else. This ties in closely with body language, because the subtle cues that our bodies emit, even when we may not be thinking about it, are far more powerful than the words that we speak. We may think we're doing all the right things, but your body language will be the one that gives you away. The only way to ensure you're entirely present during a conversation is to not have anything else distracting you.

9. Don't Interrupt

When having a conversation with someone, don't talk over or interrupt when they're speaking. Show some respect by letting the other person talk to an end before you proceed to share your thoughts and opinions. This is what makes you likable during a conversation, and it's how you win over your small talk sessions. If people like talking to you, they'll want to talk to you. This is all part of building up the skill set you need to communicate effectively. Conversation skills aren't just about knowing all the right things to say. Even if you may be excited and eager to express your views, wait until they are done speaking before you start.

10. Asking Questions That Are Open-Ended

One crucial thing that you need to be aware of is learning how to ask the right questions. The right questions are questions which are open-ended. Any item that ends in a yes or no answer is one that you should avoid. Questions should lead to answers which encourage the person you're speaking with to give longer answers, which you can use to formulate more questions and keep the conversation going. Close-ended questions are just conversation killers because they are often followed by awkward silences and neither party being sure what to say next. During your visualization sessions we talked about earlier, practice asking questions and imagine the answers that the other person might give you. This helps determine if the questions you're asking are good enough to ask when going live with someone.

11. It's Important to Keep Practicing

Great conversations don't just happen immediately after reading about the strategies you need to pull it off. Knowing the techniques are one thing, but to truly become great is going to require significant hard work and practice. Practice having conversations alone, practice having conversations with friends, even practice with strangers that you encounter daily by starting with a dull "Good morning, how are you" and see where that leads. The more you practice, the better at it you'll become, and if you're not confident just yet practicing by yourself at home in a mirror to see how you look and sound. Keep practicing using different techniques from this book and watch yourself become better with each training session.

Chapter 3 Summary

The bottom line to kickstart your conversation skills development and building some confidence along the way is to:

- Stop thinking negatively and indulging in previous low self-esteem thoughts you had about your conversational capabilities.

- Now is the time to start thinking positive and building your confidence one step at a time. Remember nobody else can do this for you, it's up to you to start.

- Visualization exercises, picture yourself as a confident and successful individual who conquers each conversation with success and assurance.

- Be prepared and arm yourself with topics of conversation to talk about, just in case you need to fall back on something when you least expect it.

- Whenever possible, prepare for small talk sessions before you begin them. This technique works well with meetings that you already expect to happen, like business meetings and networking sessions.

- Practice speaking clearly to avoid mumbling.

- Keep distractions to a minimum. Don't push it if a situation is unfavorable to engage in a small talk session due to disturbances.

- Don't interrupt the other person when they're talking. Wait until they have finished before you say what you want to say. This is the mark of a good conversationalist, allowing room for both parties to converse on equal levels.

- Be completely present, both physically and mentally, when having a conversation with someone. Your body language cues are going to let the other person know if you're distracted and not giving them your full attention.

- Practice asking the right questions. Avoid inquiries that are going to end in yes and no answers, because these are conversation killers. Open-ended questions are the way to go, and with practice, you'll become better at it as you go along.

- Practice makes perfect, knowing the skill sets is not enough. To truly master a skill requires you to practice the knowledge you've learned.

Chapter 4:

How to Become a Conversational Whiz At Work

Small talk matters more than ever at work. Business meetings, client meetings, networking sessions all rely on your ability to communicate and converse well. Without these essential skills, all your ideas and hard work won't receive the credit they deserve. You don't have to go far to see this in action either, look at the successful individuals in your work environment, your managers, and your bosses. Observe how well they can converse among themselves and to various other people they come into contact with.

Strategies You're Going to Need to Conquer Conversation at Work

You spend nine hours a day, five days a week at your workplace. This is possibly where you spend most of your waking hours if you're in full-time employment. So, it's here that your conversation skills need to shine if you want to set yourself apart from the crowd, get people to take notice of you and what you're capable of accomplishing.

1. Actively Seek Feedback

Remember Chapter Three's steps to building useful conversation skills which require practice? Your colleagues are the best people to practice on because you see them daily, and you already have to converse with them anyway, so why not use this time to practice your skills? Start actively seeking feedback from your co-workers after a conversation you've had with them. Ask them how you did and what they think you can improve upon. Let them know that you're working on developing your conversation skills at the moment, and they'll be more than happy to share what their thoughts were. It will also help you improve your relationship with them as you gradually have more things to talk about.

2. Be Someone Who Is Curious

Try to be someone who is curious about what's going on at work. That will help you to come up with the right questions to ask during a conversation. The more curious you are about your surroundings, the more information you will find that you can leverage with just about anyone in the workplace. You'll also become naturally inclined to find out more about the individuals you talk to, leading to meaningful questions and productive interactions.

3. Improve the Way You Carry Yourself

How does your personal image look like when you talk to someone? Do you stand up tall, shoulders back, full of confidence and with a smile on your face? Or are you hunched, shoulders rolled in, nervous and always wondering what people think about you? In a work environment, the way you carry yourself is just as much a part of your conversation skills as the things you say. Your body language is going to be –yet again- more potent than words. To become a great conversationalist at work, you need to mimic the air of successful people that in most cases have an open and inviting body language.

4. What's Your Tone of Voice

The workplace is an environment where the tone needs to be professional, yet friendly and approachable all at once. You may be on good terms with your colleagues, but the conversations you have still need to be kept at the appropriate professional levels. Never discuss anything that could potentially land you in hot water. Be firm without becoming aggressive by using the proper language still within professional confines.

5. Being Transparent During Your Conversations

Insufficient transparency, especially in a work environment, will only lead to one thing: people disliking you because you're perceived as someone dishonest that cannot be trusted. Being an active conversationalist means gaining the trust of the person who you are talking to so that they feel comfortable having a conversation with you. You do this by always being honest in your discussions. Don't flourish your talking points in an attempt to appear more interesting. Stick to the facts, especially when you have to work in a team. When you have a small talk with your colleagues, be open and honest about the information that you have and don't have. This helps you to gain their trust, and they'll be more inclined to engage with you in the future.

6. Pause Between Each Sentence

Work is a type of environment where we can easily get stressed, and things are always moving at a hectic pace to meet deadlines and exceed client expectations. As hectic as work can get, you still need to be in control during your small talk sessions. You do this by not feeling pressured to rush through what you're trying to say. Don't fire off one sentence after another, this makes for a pointless conversation if it's ineffective. In the earlier chapters, you remember how rushing through information is going to backfire on you because you could miss delivering essential details. Being a great conversationalist means that you are the one in control of the conversation, you have the power to make it meaningful. Even in a pressured setting, avoid rushing through your sentences. A discussion is always more effective when the message is clearly delivered and received.

7. Don't Let Emotions Rule You

Sometimes emotions can run high, understandable given all the stress and how much goes on at work. But you know what successful conversationalists don't do? They don't wear their emotions on their sleeve, especially if they aren't the most positive and optimistic ones. A good conversationalist is one firmly in control of their mental state during a conversation. This is going to take some practice, but a great tip is to remind yourself to focus on your breathing. Take deep breaths, and tell yourself it's okay, that you can handle anything that comes your way. Avoid responding with the first thing that comes to your mind, especially in a heated situation where you're more likely to say the wrong things. Also, remember to watch your tone of voice and the way you respond.

8. Get Rid of Any Nervous Characteristics You May Have

If you have any particular traits giving away how nervous you are when engaging in small talk with someone, now is the time to get rid of those. Are you fidgety during a conversation because you're nervous? Are you tapping your feet or your fingers excessively? Do you twiddle your fingers or make nervous gesturing with your hands whenever you're conversing with someone? Do you avoid eye contact? If you've been guilty of doing all these things in the past, starting from today, kick those nervous mannerisms out the door because there is no room for them in the new and improved you. From now on, be conscious of your body when you're about to begin a conversation. Before you walk up to them, stand up tall, roll your shoulders back and smile before taking confident strides towards them and introducing yourself (if you're meeting them for the first time). Relax your body while you're talking to them, and make a quick, conscious survey of yourself to make sure you're not falling back on any nervous behaviors. This may take time and practice to nail down before you become comfortable enough.

Chapter 4 Summary

Here are the strategies you want to keep up your sleeve to help conquer conversation at work:

- Be someone who is naturally curious about your surroundings and the people you are conversing with. This will help you to ask for more in-depth and meaningful questions which tend to improve the effectiveness of a conversational session.

- Actively seek feedback from your colleagues about how your conversation skills are, and what they think needs to be improved on. Practice your small talk strategies and conversation skills on your co-workers and ask them how they thought you were doing.

- Carry yourself with confidence and try to stand up tall, smile, be approachable, and speak openly. Strive to be someone who is confident about and know what to say.

- Using the right tone of voice at work is just as important as the things that you say. Try to find the balance between maintaining an air of professionalism, yet being friendly and approachable at the same time.

- Be honest and transparent in any conversation you have at work. Hiding information or not being upfront about something is only going to make your colleagues and clients dislike and distrust you.

- Don't rush through your sentences even if you are pressed for time. A conversation is more meaningful when a message is both delivered and received clearly. You cannot achieve this if all you're doing is making the other person feel uncomfortable and rushed when you're talking to them.

- Don't let your emotions rule you during a conversation (both at work and everyday life). Pause for a second and fight your immediate reaction to respond right away to avoid saying the wrong things.

- Forget your previous nervous mannerisms, there's no place for them if you want to become a great conversationalist.

Chapter 5:

Charismatically Cool

Knowing what to say, how to say it and when to say it is all the marks of a great conversationalist. But there's something else added into the mix to become a master of small talk. What else do you notice about successful individuals?

They're charismatic.

They seem to have this ability to draw people in when they are talking, especially motivational speakers like Tony Robbins and Les Brown. They seem to enrapture you from the moment they begin speaking. That's charisma at work. Some people are born with the natural gift of appeal, while others have to work at developing it. It's often mistaken as part of a person's character, but it's a skill that you can acquire.

Just like confidence, it's going to take time and practice to build charisma, but if you persist and keep at it, you're going to get there eventually. Before you can start working on your charming nature, you first need to:

Become a Master of Conversational Basics

Before you can begin working on your charisma, you need to work on building up the foundations of your conversational skills, using the techniques talked about in the earlier chapters. If you carefully observe individuals who are charismatic, they seem to know just how to talk to people, how to start a conversation, how to keep it going, how to steer it in the direction they want and how to command people's attention with the things they say. They have mastered the basics.

You must first work and practice on developing your small talk skills. It's only when you have become confident enough in those abilities that you should move onto the next phase of charisma development.

1. You Must Learn to Smile

And don't make it forced. A charismatic person's smile is relaxed, natural and at ease, warm, genuine and friendly. This is the smile you need to project during your conversations with people. Smiling instantly makes the other person feel more calm and comfortable during the discussion. When you smile, you appear more likable, and a genuine smile that lights up your face makes the other person smile back at you. A sincere smile is an essential quality you need to have as a charismatic person. Practice smiling to yourself in front of a mirror daily, try to feel relaxed and happy when you do it and observe how it turns out. Does it look natural enough? Does it seem stiff or forced in any way? The best way to project a genuine smile during a small talk session is to want to engage with the person. When you want to do something, it no longer feels like it's a forced thing that you have to do.

2. Manage Just the Right Amount of Eye Contact

You want to be looking at the person you're talking to, but not staring them down like you're trying to challenge or intimidate them. Eye contact is critical to establish during a conversation because it lets the other person know that they are worthy of your attention, that you're entirely focused and interested in everything that they have to say. Have you ever been in a conversation where the person was distracted or looking around everywhere else but at you during a conversation? It can be infuriating and almost disrespectful! The best eye contact length to maintain is to hold a person's gaze for one second longer than you would typically do. Practice keeping eye contact during your small talk practice sessions, keep the person's gaze a bit longer, and then briefly look elsewhere without turning your head away when you blink. Practice doing this in front of the mirror, practice when you greet people in the morning, with your colleagues at work, with the cashier who is checking out your groceries. There are many opportunities for you to practice; you just have to start utilizing them until you get good at it.

3. Don't Be Stiff

Charismatic people are expressive with their bodies, but not to a point where it goes overboard. They don't stand there during a conversation looking stiff as a board with their arms firmly by their sides. That's what uncomfortable people do, and what you should aim to avoid. You need to be relaxed during a conversation, and gesture with just the right amount to express enthusiasm, but not to a point where you're going overboard with it. When you're practicing small talk in front of a mirror, notice the way you gesture. Are you nodding far too much? Are your hands moving around too enthusiastically? Little gestures like these may not seem like much to you, but they could be perceived differently by other people. Some people may not like it, some may be put off by it, and some may find it uncomfortable to be around you. After you've practiced by yourself in front of a mirror a couple of times, ask some friends for some feedback about how you come across when you're talking. Are you doing too much of something? Are you not doing enough? Try to get different perspectives and honest opinions, that way you can make a note of what you need to keep practicing on and what you're already doing well. It also helps to watch videos of motivational speakers and talks given by successful individuals to see just how they do it and try to mimic that.

4. Be Witty

One of the best traits of a charismatic person is how they can make other people laugh without appearing like they try too hard. The humor just seems to flow naturally as part of the conversation, and like everything else that a charismatic person does, it appears almost effortless. People love individuals who can make them laugh. To become more charismatic you need to become someone who can make others laugh without trying too hard, that's the key. You can learn to be charming and to develop a sense of humor by first learning how to laugh at yourself. Being able to do that lets others know that you are confident and comfortable enough in your own skin, that you don't mind if people join in and laugh right along with you. Being able to laugh at yourself without feeling uncomfortable is the first step. You can then learn how to attune yourself to what other people's humor is like, which usually happens after you've had a conversation with them several times. Gauge your audience to know the type of jokes which are acceptable. For example, if you are around a group of people who are more sensitive or reserved by nature, then it's better to first be observant and hold back on the jokes, so you don't risk offending anyone. Don't try too hard to be funny either by feeling pressured to make a laugh every time. Choose your moments and when the opportunity comes up, use it.

5. Make the Person You're Talking to Feel Special

Conquering small talk means being so good of a conversationalist that you can make the people you are talking to feel special, valued and that their opinions and ideas matter. It's actually quite simple to do; you just have to start by being respectful. You need to treat everyone like an equal, and nobody should be beneath or above you. Show each person you're talking to respect, and show them that you're interested and keen on what they have to say. Ask questions to invite them to open up or share their thoughts on specific subjects. Listen attentively when they are talking and show the appropriate reactions when called for, for example, nodding your head when you agree and making brief interjections to assure them that you are listening. Brief interjections could be along the lines of *I see,* or *I agree with that* depending on how your conversation is going.

And finally, remember that there's a difference between being a charismatic person and being someone who is a people-pleaser. You want people to like you and find you charming, but you don't want to be someone who bends over at everyone's will. People who are charismatic are confident about themselves, and they get people to like them for their own personalities. If someone doesn't like you, that's okay since you can't get along with everyone in this world.

Chapter 5 Summary

To develop that natural charm that people seem to gravitate towards, here is what you need to do to become more charismatic:

- The first and most important step is to keep practicing your small talk skills until you have become a master of the basics. When you can communicate and converse well with just about anyone – and not just the people you are comfortable with - then you are well and truly ready to begin working on your charisma.

- Smile genuinely and warmly during a conversation, it makes you appear more charismatic.

- Start practicing maintaining good eye contact at every opportunity you get. Remember the mark of the perfect eye contact is to hold a person's gaze for just one second longer than you usually would and go with that.

- Don't stand uncomfortably during a conversation, you need to be aware of how your body is behaving. Charismatic people know how to display enthusiasm without going overboard, and you need to practice doing the same. If it helps, watch videos online of some successful people you admire and observe their body movements when they're talking to a crowd.

- Learn to be witty, but don't try too hard to be funny. Let the joke come naturally and flow smoothly with the conversation. A well-timed joke is superior to a forced one.

- Make the other person you're talking to feel special by showing them you are interested in what they have to say, and that their ideas and opinions matter to you.

Chapter 6:

Conversational Confidence Is Key

Confidence is crucial for every conversationalist. It will be hard without it to convince people to believe in you when you don't even believe in yourself. Even if you have every strategy for success at your disposal, if you don't have the confidence to back it up, it's going to be all for nothing.

Why Is Confidence So Important?

Here is what happens when you lack the confidence to pull off small talk (or anything else in general for that matter, not just about a social interaction):

1. Fear Will Always Be What Holds You Back

If you're regularly ruled by fear and anxiety of everything that could go wrong, there will be many things that you don't do or try. You become so afraid of failing that you fail to do anything at all, even if it something that would benefit you in the long run.

Something as simple as walking up to someone and saying *Hello, how are you?* can be challenging to manage since you're so afraid of being embarrassed.

2. You're Going to Miss Out on Opportunities

Especially at work where small talk is a potential networking opportunity that could lead to bigger and better things for your career. Missing out and letting them pass you by is linked closely with the point above, that same fear is going to stop you and make you hesitant about grabbing opportunities right in front of you. In life, it could prevent you from forging new friendships, relationships and more.

3. You'll Find It Hard to be Happy

Someone who is lacking confidence generally has feelings of low self-esteem, and they are always thinking about their flaws which makes it hard for them to be happy. When all you can think about is your inadequacies, how are you going to concentrate on everything you are supposed to do to be better? Negativity is a powerful emotion, one that comes much more easily than positivity.

How to Become a More Confident Person

Do you see how much insufficient confidence can affect you? Confidence is vital, especially when making an impression on someone during a small talk session. Being confident gives you the courage to know that you can manage the situation you are in, that you can control how a conversation is going.

1. Mind Over Matter

Confidence begins in your mind, and it's a state of mind that you and only you have the power to change. You must want to change the way you think about yourself, and let go of negative connotations you associate with. There are plenty of ways you can help strengthen your mindset over time. Tell yourself that *you are* a confident person who is more than capable of handling anything that comes your way. One way of doing this, for example, is through meditation, a good exercise for the mind, body, and soul. Another way is through affirmations or writing it down on little post-it notes and sticking it in places which you can easily see, continually surrounding yourself with messages of positive reinforcement. Again, it's about finding what works best for you, but try to start strengthening your mind to think more positively.

2. Identify What You Need to Work On

Self-doubt is one of the most significant mental obstacles to overcome when it comes to building confidence in yourself and what you're capable of. You've been saddled with self-doubt for perhaps a long time, it can almost seem impossible to think in any other way. It will be a struggle in the beginning, but it must be done if you want to begin developing and transforming into a better version of yourself. Begin by making a list of what you think are the areas you need to work on. Once you're done, proceed to make a list of possible suggestions about what you can do to improve those areas. It doesn't necessarily have to be massive, drastic changes all at once. It won't do you any good if you're feeling overwhelmed. Start small and put achievable goals that you can accomplish and keep repeating that process once you start completing them.

3. Acknowledge What You Have Done Well

Did you handle something particularly well today? Even better than you thought? It's time to start acknowledging it. Make it a habit from today and onward to recognize and congratulate yourself on a job well done each time you've made an accomplishment. After all, it's an achievement, and every achievement deserves recognition. For example, if you had a particularly successful small talk session today, fantastic work! Great job. Treat yourself to something good as a reward. You should be proud of what you have accomplished which also helps to build your confidence slowly over time.

4. Make a List of Your Strengths

Sometimes, it's easier to believe something when you see it written down in front of you. If you're having trouble making a list of your pros, enlist the help of family and friends to do it. Ask them to tell you what they admire the most about you, and what they think you're good at. Ask them to help you identify what your strengths are. It can help boost your confidence too, knowing that this is what other people think about you, things that you may not even have thought about. Once you've compiled your list, go through it daily until you firmly believe in each point written down and you feel an increase in your confidence level.

5. You Need to Look Good to Feel Good

The way you look and feel about yourself is going to make a difference in your confidence levels. How much time do you spend taking care of your appearance and the way you present yourself? Is your hair neatly fixed? Do you wear clothes that fit well? The way you look is going to be the first thing that people will notice about you when you introduce yourself and taking some time to look and feel your best will help. You don't have to buy a new wardrobe to look the part, just work with what you have right now. Make sure your clothes always look clean, are comfortable and that they make you feel good. The better you feel about yourself, the more confident you will be.

Chapter 6 Summary

Confidence is an important part that *you need to work on* to become a better conversationalist:

- It's about mind over matter, and it's entirely in your hands to start changing your mindset. One example of how you can do this is either through positive affirmations or even meditation, but you should find a way that works best for you to get the most effective results.

- Congratulate yourself when you've done something well. It doesn't necessarily have to be significant accomplishments. Even the little things you achieved during the day that makes you say *I did it!* are good. Acknowledging when you've accomplished something well will help you to gradually build confidence over time.

- Identify the areas you need to work on for improvement and make a list of possible suggestions you can do to better those areas. It doesn't have to be massive goals. Start with small achievable ones you can accomplish, so you don't end up feeling discouraged.

- Make a list of your strengths which acts as evidence about what positive traits you have that you can utilize. You may not have noticed or thought about these before, but use them to help regain and build confidence.

- Devote some time to personal hygiene and taking care of your clothes. Ensure that you feel good about yourself before leaving the house, this will help to build your confidence.

Conclusion

You now have everything you need and more to start practicing on improving your conversation skills and becoming better at small talk. It may take time and effort, but if you keep practicing, eventually, you will get there. It's not a skill or technique you need to be born with, it's not an exceptional talent you need to possess to become good. Learning great conversation skills is something that everyone can do.

All it takes is practice. Start practicing the techniques you have learned in this book and putting them into practice at every opportunity you get. The more you practice, the better you'll become and one day, you'll master the art of small talk. As your conversation skills start to improve, you will notice that your confidence in conversing with people also enhances in tandem. With enough practice, you'll have the ability to hold a conversation with anyone, even complete strangers.

9 789198 569148